Since Childhood

Memories from the Life of the Martyr Muḥammad al-Jawād Ḥijāzī "Sayyid Bāqir"

I0517948

Rīm ʿAllāw

AL-BURĀQ

Copyright

ISBN: 978-1-956276-58-9
Printed and published by al-Burāq Publications.
Translated and annotated by al-Burāq Publications. Where needed, context and transliterations were added. Some minor edits were made to the translated text.

www.al-Buraq.org
publications@al-Buraq.org

First Edition | December 2024

Dedication

The publication of this book was made possible through the generous support of our donors.

Please recite *Sūrat al-Fātihah* and ask God for the Divine reward (*thawāb*) to be conferred upon the donors and also the souls of all the deceased in whose memory their loved ones have contributed graciously towards the publication of *Since Childhood: Memories from the Life of the Martyr Muḥammad al-Jawād Ḥijāzī.*

We begin by giving all praise and thanks to God ﷻ for giving us the *tawfīq* to translate this book. He has guided us and without Him, we would not have been guided to the straight path embodied by the Prophet Muḥammad ﷺ and the Ahl al-Bayt عليهم السلام.

This book is dedicated to all the scholars, martyrs and believers who worked tirelessly to promote the pure Muḥammadan path.

We want to also give our thanks and appreciation to all believers from around the world and acknowledge the team which helped al-Burāq Publications complete this work, spending countless hours to make its publication possible. Please recite Sūrat al-Fātiḥah on behalf of them, their families, and their marḥūmīn.

Lastly, this book is dedicated in honor of Shahīd Muḥammad al-Jawād Ḥijāzī and his family. Please remember them in your prayers and may God ﷻ have mercy on them and their loved ones.

Duʿāʾ al-Ḥujjah

اللهم كن لوليك الحجة بن الحسن صلواتك

عليه وعلى آبائه في هذه الساعة وفي كل

ساعة وليا وحافظا وقائدا وناصرا ودليلا

وعينا حتى تسكنه أرضك طوعا وتمتعه فيها طويلا

O God, be, for Your representative, the Ḥujjat (proof), son of al-Ḥasan, Your blessings be upon him and his forefathers, in this hour and in every hour: a guardian, a protector, a leader, a helper, a proof, and an eye—until You make him live on the Earth, in obedience (to You), and cause him to live in it for a long time.

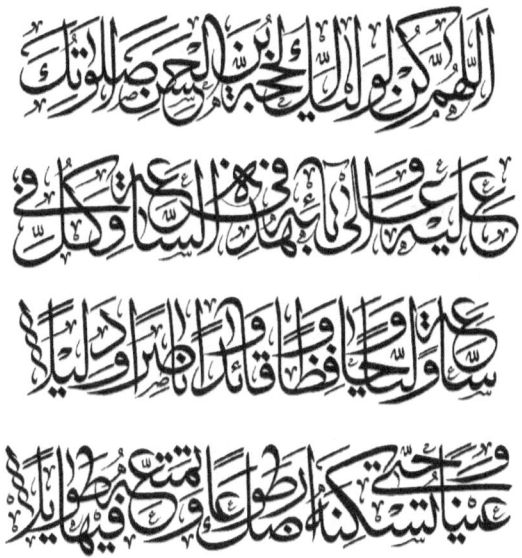

Terms of Respect

The following Arabic phrases have been used throughout this book in their respective places to show the reverence which the noble personalities deserve.

عزّ وجلّ

Used for God, meaning:
Exalted and Sublime (Perfect) is He

صلى الله عليه وآله

Used for Prophet Muḥammad, meaning:
Blessings from God be upon him and his family

عليه السلام

Used for a man (singular) of a high status, meaning:
Peace be upon him

عليها السلام

Used for a woman (singular) of a high status, meaning:
Peace be upon her

عليهما السلام

Used for men/women (dual) of a high status, meaning:
Peace be upon them both

عليهم السلام

Used for men and/or women (plural) of a high status, meaning:
Peace be upon them all

عجّل الله تعالى فرجه الشريف

Used for Imām Muḥammad al-Mahdī, meaning:
May God hasten his return

قدّس سرّه

Used for a deceased scholar, meaning:
May his resting [burial] place remain pure

Transliteration Table

The method of transliteration of Islāmic terminology from the Arabic language has been carried out according to the standard transliteration table below.

ء	ʾ	ر	r	ف	f
ا	a	ز	z	ق	q
ب	b	س	s	ك	k
ت	t	ش	sh	ل	l
ث	th	ص	ṣ	م	m
ج	j	ض	ḍ	ن	n
ح	ḥ	ط	ṭ	و	w
خ	kh	ظ	ẓ	ه	h
د	d	ع	ʿ	ي	y
ذ	dh	غ	gh		
Long Vowels					
ا	ā	و	ū	ي	ī
Short Veowels					
ـَـ	a	ـُـ	u	ـِـ	i

Table of Contents

Disclaimer

This publication is not affiliated with, influenced by, or funded by any domestic or foreign political entities. It is intended purely for historical record-keeping due to the lack of accessible Arabic texts for a Western audience. This text is aimed at academics and historians alike, providing valuable insights into the subject matter. The contents do not represent our views or opinions, nor do they endorse any specific ideologies or perspectives presented. While every effort has been made to ensure the accuracy and relevance of the selected texts, the publication may not include all viewpoints. The material reflects the historical context at the time of writing and should be understood as such.

بسم الله الرحمن الرحيم

﴿وَلَا تَحْسَبَنَّ ٱلَّذِينَ قُتِلُوا۟ فِى سَبِيلِ ٱللَّهِ
أَمْوَٰتًۢا ۚ بَلْ أَحْيَآءٌ عِندَ رَبِّهِمْ يُرْزَقُونَ﴾

﴿wa-lā taḥsabanna lladhīna qutilū fī sabīli llāhi ʾamwātan bal ʾaḥyāʾun ʿinda rabbihim yurzaqūn[a]*﴾*

﴿Do not suppose those who were slain in the way of God to be dead; no, they are living and provided for near their Lord﴾[1]

---

[1] Sūrat Āl ʿImrān, Verse 169.

بسم الله الرحمن الرحيم

﴿وَلَا تَقُولُوا۟ لِمَن يُقْتَلُ فِى سَبِيلِ ٱللَّهِ أَمْوَٰتٌۢ ۚ
بَلْ أَحْيَآءٌ وَلَٰكِن لَّا تَشْعُرُونَ﴾

﴾wa-lā taqūlū li-man yuqtalu fī sabīli llāhi
ʾamwātun bal ʾaḥyāʾun wa-lākin
lā tashʿurūna﴿

﴾Do not call those who were slain in God's
way 'dead.' No, they are living,
but you are not aware﴿[2]

---

[2] Sūrat al-Baqarah, Verse 154.

Introduction

بسم الله الرحمن الرحيم

In the Name of God, the Beneficent, the Merciful

On Friday, March 6, I came across an article by the mother of Martyr Muḥammad al-Jawād Ḥijāzī. In this article, she spoke about a new dignity for the martyr related to fulfilling the needs of one of the sisters after his martyrdom.

I observed the extent of people's engagement with the article's topic, witnessed their intense love for the martyr, and read numerous comments in which they discussed their connection with Martyr Muḥammad, seeking his intercession when beseeching God ﷻ. This did not surprise me, as I knew how pure and faithful he was.

I decided to write some fragments of his virtuous life, with the help of his dear mother, to let people know more about him and spread the morals of the great martyrs.

I spoke with his mother and requested her assistance in compiling this book. She was delighted with the idea and warmly welcomed it.

> When I went to sleep that night, I saw Muḥammad al-Jawād in my dreams. His face was beaming with joy and contentment. He approached me, and I told him:

> Muḥammad, I will start writing about you; are you pleased?

At that moment, he responded,

> Yes, I am pleased. However, be attentive to the intricacies of your writing and conduct extensive research. You will uncover many stories that you are unaware of. Search, search...

Indeed, I faced many challenges in completing. This was primarily due to his determination to keep his religious activities, worship, and personal matters private. Everything documented here was a result of coincidence, particularly because the martyr was reserved when it came to discussing his affairs.

Meeting the request of Martyr Muḥammad al-Jawād Ḥijāzī, the book was named *Since Childhood*. Ḥajj ʿAbbās, the martyr's father, had visited the grave of his beloved son and asked him about the title that should be chosen for the book. Five days later, his response came to his father through a dream. It showed that Martyr Muḥammad was still alive—his physical body was buried in the ground, but his soul was still present and receiving sustenance from God. Coming from the war fronts, Muḥammad asked his mother to wake up and put food for him. His mother responded to his request in company with Ḥajj ʿAbbās. When dinner ended, both Ḥajj ʿAbbās and Ḥajjah Ḥawrāʾ went to rest a bit in their room. After a while, Ḥajj ʿAbbās came up and looked at Muḥammad al-Jawād; he was surprised to see his son as a 10-year-old. When Ḥajj ʿAbbās narrated the dream, he said Muḥammad al-Jawād wanted him to name the book *Since Childhood.*

The same night, the martyr's brother's wife saw in her dream that Ḥajj ʿAbbās was sending her photos of a 5-year-old Muḥammad al-Jawād with a long beard. Astonished, she remarked:

> Grace be to God since you were young; your features were that of the Shuhadāʾ.

Muḥammad al-Jawād chose this as the book's title, and the second dream reinforced his choice. After his martyrdom, an epitaph poem, starting with *Since Childhood*, was gifted to him. It is translated and found at the end of this book.

In summary, Muḥammad al-Jawād's secret started in childhood.

We often aspire to emulate the morals and ethics of the Imāms عليهم السلام, yet we may encounter challenges in delving into the intricate details of their biographies. Not everyone may find the time for such in-depth study.

To gain a deeper understanding of the Imāms عليهم السلام, we can turn to the stories of the martyrs who have followed in their footsteps.

We do not intend to overlook or exclude the stories of the Ahl al-Bayt عليهم السلام in any way. However, it is noticeable that the Imāms عليهم السلام profoundly influenced many martyrs. By exploring the biography of Martyr Muḥammad al-Jawād and observing his strong connection with Abū al-Faḍl al-'Abbās, we can expedite our understanding of the Imāms ﷺ. Every martyr's life is marked by the ethical teachings of the Ahl al-Bayt ﷺ.

Everything recorded about Muḥammad al-Jawād falls short of capturing the essence of the bloodshed. However, our unwavering loyalty to his pure blood motivates us to write and introduce people to the depth of his purity and faith. His martyrdom has left a deep pain in the heart and a void that can only be filled by meeting him. The voices of his comrades in jihād[3] (a struggle against the enemy, or foremost with one's soul) tremble when they speak of him, rendering words inadequate.

I say to you, O Muḥammad, we are students in your school. Just as your companions asked you not to forget them and to guide them, I implore you to include me in your prayers, O Jawād. Do not forget us; visit us frequently. Lead us toward goodness and righteousness.

In conclusion, this book's contents are derived from the recollections of the martyr's mother and his esteemed family and brothers in jihād. May God ﷻ reward them abundantly. I deeply appreciate and thank them.

---

[3] A struggle against one's enemy (jihād al-aṣghar, the lesser jihād) or, more significantly, a struggle against oneself (jihād al-akbar, the greater jihād).

The Words of the Martyr's Mother

I was brought up upon the path of Ahl al-Bayt ‿ and wilāyah. Hence, since childhood, I participated in commemorations for several martyrs, amongst them the Leader of the Martyrs of the Resistance, Sayyid 'Abbās[4]. During my life, I thought I knew the meaning of martyrdom. Until the martyrdom of Muḥammad, my understanding of martyrdom changed. I understood the true meaning of love for God ‿. I came to understand the secret to why the young men at the prime of their youth gave up the world (dunyā) with all its temptations, how they sell their minds to God ‿, and how they completely submit the soul and mind to the Eternal Lover.

I was raised to embrace the path of Ahl al-Bayt ‿ and the concept of wilāyah. From my early years, I actively participated in commemorations honoring various martyrs, including the esteemed Leader of the Resistance, Sayyid 'Abbās. However, it was not until a certain period in my life, marked by the martyrdom of Muḥammad, that my comprehension of martyrdom underwent a profound transformation. Then, I truly grasped the essence of love for God ‿. I uncovered the hidden wisdom behind why these young men, in the prime of their youth, relinquish

---

[4] Sayyid 'Abbās al-Mūsawī (1952–1992) was a prominent Shī'ī cleric, Islāmic scholar, and leader. He is remembered for his dedication to the principles of the Ahl al-Bayt ‿ and his significant role in Lebanon's Resistance against occupation. His efforts combined religious guidance with political and military leadership to defend his people's sovereignty and dignity and fight oppression.

worldly temptations, essentially selling their minds to God ﷻ and wholeheartedly surrendering their souls and intellect to the Eternal Beloved.

I understood the meaning of the saying that the world is fleeting and the meaning of jihād with sincerity and certainty. My son teaches me lessons with his martyrdom, which universities worldwide fail to teach (or which no university in the world will ever be able to teach). The Qur'ānic verse

﴿وَلَا تَقُولُوا۟ لِمَن يُقْتَلُ فِي سَبِيلِ ٱللَّهِ أَمْوَٰتٌۢ بَلْ أَحْيَآءٌ وَلَٰكِن لَّا تَشْعُرُونَ﴾

﴿wa-lā taqūlū li-man yuqtalu fī sabīli llāhi 'amwātun bal 'aḥyā'un wa-lākin lā tash'urūna﴾

﴿Do not call those who were slain in God's way 'dead.' No, they are living, but you are not aware﴾[5]

was expressed before my eyes.

Since my son's martyrdom until today, I did not feel for a single moment that he was absent, but his presence increased even more. His shadow is with me at all times (or all the time). His smile, which never left his face one day in this world, still fills my life with joy and happiness, and it has increased in brightness and glow. You might be surprised by how my life has transformed, brimming with increased joy and happiness since his martyrdom. Because if you look at it from a worldly perspective, life after

---

[5] Sūrat al-Baqarah, Verse 154.

martyrdom would be considered dark and full of grief for me. However, I look at life from a God-centered perspective.

I bore witness to the events of Karbalā' and the sacrifices of Ahl al-Bayt ﷺ, where lives were offered in the path of the ﷻ. It was a profound awakening of the spirit and the soul. As I beheld the epitome of patience, Sayyidah Zaynab ﷺ, I did not merely perceive her through the eyes of my heart; I saw how she turned her family's martyrdom and captivity into a testament of resilience and beauty.

In the eyes of God ﷻ, my son Muḥammad al-Jawād bestowed upon me the most precious gift that only a truly blessed mother could receive. He granted me honor and pride, not just in this world but also in the Hereafter. Through his deeds, he adorned my presence in the company of the Sayyidat Nisā' al-'Ālamīn (Lady of the Women of the Worlds, Sayyidah Fāṭimah al-Zahrā' ﷺ), whom I hold in the highest esteem (may my soul be sacrificed for her).

How can I not thank God ﷻ and remain patient after all this giving? Muḥammad al-Jawād was a mi'rāj for me[6] with the supplication in which I recite,

> O God, change my bad condition [or state of hardship] into the best (or a better) condition.

---

[6] In the sense of meeting him in the sense of it being an ascension, as it facilitated a heightened state of faith, understanding, and spiritual transformation

And now I am in my best condition because I saw nothing but beauty.

Ziyārah al-Shuhadāʾ

السَّلَامُ عَلَيْكُمْ يَا أَوْلِيَاءَ اللَّهِ وَأَحِبَّاءَهُ

Peace be upon you, O allies of God and His beloved ones

السَّلَامُ عَلَيْكُمْ يَا أَصْفِيَاءَ اللَّهِ وَأَوِدَّاءَهُ

Peace be upon you, O select ones of God and His supporters

السَّلَامُ عَلَيْكُمْ يَا أَنْصَارَ دِينِ اللَّهِ

Peace be upon you, O supporters of the religion of God

السَّلَامُ عَلَيْكُمْ يَا أَنْصَارَ رَسُولِ اللَّهِ

Peace be upon you, O supporters of the Messenger of God

السَّلَامُ عَلَيْكُمْ يَا أَنْصَارَ أَمِيرِ الْمُؤْمِنِينَ

Peace be upon you, O supporters of the Commander of the Faithful

السَّلَامُ عَلَيْكُمْ يَا أَنْصَارَ فَاطِمَةَ سَيِّدَةِ نِسَاءِ الْعَالَمِينَ

Peace be upon you, O supporters of Fāṭimah, the Lady of the Women of the Worlds

السَّلَامُ عَلَيْكُمْ يَا أَنْصَارَ أَبِي مُحَمَّدٍ الْحَسَنِ بْنِ عَلِيٍّ الْوَلِيِّ النَّاصِحِ

Peace be upon you, O supporters of Abū Muḥammad al-Ḥasan bin ʿAlī, the loyal guardian

السَّلَامُ عَلَيْكُمْ يَا أَنْصَارَ أَبِي عَبْدِ اللَّهِ

Peace be upon you, O supporters of Abū ʿAbdullāh

بِأَبِي أَنْتُمْ وَأُمِّي طِبْتُمْ وَطَابَتْ الْأَرْضُ الَّتِي فِيهَا دُفِنْتُمْ

By my father and my mother, you are blessed, and blessed is the land in which you are buried

وَفُزْتُمْ فَوْزًا عَظِيمًا

You have achieved a great success

فَيَا لَيْتَنِي كُنْتُ مَعَكُمْ فَأَفُوزَ مَعَكُمْ

Oh, how I wish I were with you, so that I could achieve success with you.

The Best of Stories Part One

Sūrat Yūsuf has been named 'The Best of Stories' as it starts with a dream and ends with its interpretation. We will also start this book with the narration of a dream that Muḥammad al-Jawād had twenty days before his martyrdom, and we will interpret it in the final pages of this book. Just as Prophet Yūsuf ﷺ narrated the dream himself, we will narrate it in the words of Muḥammad al-Jawād when he narrated it to his mother.

****

In my dream, I saw a young man standing at the end of the road, surrounded by a halo of bright light. When I came closer, I realized he was my friend, Martyr Ḥasan Sallūm. As usual, his smiling face overwhelmed me as if I was facing a spot of light. I saw the road right before my eyes; I held my breath as I walked it, with my eyes wide open until I reached its end.

I ended up in front of a car with blinding lights illuminating its door openings. I gently opened the door and went inside. I reclined in the car seat and looked at my side, which made the view more beautiful. Suddenly, a man appeared inside the car. His features were slowly revealed: a gleaming, beautiful face, a black turban on his head, and a black cloak on his shoulders. I knew he was the "Custodian of Blood," the Martyred Sayyid.

I moved closer to his eminence and caressed his immaculate chin. He did not utter a word; his presence and warm smile were more eloquent than any words. He took off his turban and gave it to me, then patted my head with his blessed hand. I knew then that I was being cared for in a way no man would have imagined.

I woke up confused as if I had been moved from an orbit to an orbit and from a resurrection to a resurrection. I felt like I was caught between my soul's sentiment and the worlds of yesterday and tomorrow. I felt I had been chosen for a divinely fated matter that would come true.

With confusion and worry, I told my mom about this dream.

The Cradle

In the eyes of Muḥammad al-Jawād, a bright light made his parents realize that he was seeing the world from a different perspective. His eyes had a sparkle that penetrated the veils of imagination and, at other times, received the awaited hints of perpetuity. Since birth, the light of his eyes has a sparkle that captures the one who looks at him. Wonderful, he was among the children! One of the most prominent characteristics distinguishing him from the others was that he was a fan of silence and a lover of gazing. His mother, Ḥajjah Ḥawrā' al-Riz, says that when she checked on him every night, she would find him awake in his cradle, observing the things around him. The child with wide eyes reveals secrets that the tongue cannot utter. Muḥammad al-Jawād was an enlightened being who sought martyrdom from the moment he was born. Isn't the rose a flower from when the seed was planted? Martyrdom is just like it, for a martyr is a martyr from the moment of his birth.

In 1992, the pure Ḥusaynī house welcomed with great joy the first child of their children. On December 6, Muḥammad al-Jawād Ḥijāzī was born, and he opened his eyes for the first time in Brazil. He was born in the year of Sayyid 'Abbās's martyrdom; may his soul be sanctified. His parents took many pictures of him, with pictures of Sayyid 'Abbās. Thus, Muḥammad al-Jawād planted the seeds of Martyr 'Abbās's love in himself from childhood.

Muḥammad al-Jawād grew up in a family that urged the observance of religious concepts. His father, Ḥajj 'Abbās Ḥijāzī, was diligent concerning religious rulings and encouraged moral concepts. As for his mother, Ḥajjah

Ḥawrāʾ al-Riz had a major role in his upbringing, and her good morals and character greatly influenced him. His upbringing began in the bosom of his mother, who was his first school; then, he graduated with a high degree in conduct, behavior, and morals.

When he reached the age of 10, he moved with his family to Lebanon (Lubnān) and continued his scientific and jihādi life until he was blessed by God ﷻ and joined the ranks of the martyrs on January 31, 2016, in Syria (Sūrīyah)—Idlib, Sahl al-Ghab.

He chose Bāqir al-Mūsawī as his title, but he is better known as Sayyid Bāqir. Muḥammad al-Jawād drank a pure Mūsawī drink during his first and second births.

He Has Made Me Kind

Upholding Dutifulness to My Mother

The son is comforted by his mother's presence and gets along with her without the need for others. The loving bond between them is considered instinctive and does not need evidence. From a psychological perspective, a mother represents a source of affection and tenderness that every child naturally seeks. Unsurprisingly, the boy rushed toward his mother and got along with her in spirit, heart, and mind.

Muḥammad al-Jawād was immersed in his loving mother's emotions. He was the beat in the heart of a mother full of compassion for her children. There existed a profound and mutual respect between Muḥammad al-Jawād and his mother. He perceived her through two lenses: one of appreciation and respect and the other as his confidante and friend, the keeper of his secrets in the sanctuary of their home.

Ḥajjah Ḥawrāʾ narrates:

Ḥajj ʿAbbās frequently traveled due to the nature of his work. On one occasion, he left Lubnān (Lebanon) for a job, and my children and I became accustomed to living alone until his return. However, a few days after his departure, I fell ill. With three children to care for, I could not visit a doctor. I attempted to conceal my fatigue and not display it in front of the children, but my condition worsened to the point where I could neither speak nor move.

Muḥammad al-Jawād responded urgently in this vulnerable state, embodying a mother's concern about her child. I sensed his fear, as though our roles had reversed, and he had become the caregiver. He repeatedly inquired,

Are you okay? Can I get you anything?

I asked him to put on his shoes and bring some water that had the Noble Qur'ān recited over it from our neighbor. Before I could finish my sentence, he hurried to fulfill my request. In just two minutes, he returned, holding the cup of water with his small hands. I distinctly recall that on that day, he remained by my side until I felt better. It is not an exaggeration to describe him as a kind mother; his tenderness reflects a mother's care. I also witnessed his attentive service when I was hit by a car and broke my leg. He continued to care for me with the gentleness of his eyes, never leaving me alone.

The days went by, and the holy month of Ramaḍān arrived; one night, after breaking our fast, Muḥammad al-Jawād decided to go out and spend some time with his brother and friends. Before leaving, he approached me, kissed my cheek, and asked if I needed anything. He repeated his question several times. He stood at the house door, moving back and forth as if he did not want to leave us alone out of fear that we would get bored. At that moment, I understood what was going on in his mind. I asked him to go out without being concerned about us. Even though it was his right to go out for an evening stroll, his constant consideration and concern for us, especially me, came from within his heart; it held a special charm.

****

At that time, Muḥammad al-Jawād was twelve years old, and Maḥmūd was ten years old. They were playing downstairs in the building.

While playing, they found a gold bracelet. They brought the bracelet to me, saying,

> Mother, look, we found it inside the building. Perhaps one of the women dropped it.

I suggested they put a note inside the elevator, stating that if someone had lost something, they should come to our house. However, we did not mention the specific item on the note to ensure its safety.

Later that day, the doorbell rang, and it was the mother of one of our neighbors. She said she had lost a gold bracelet and described it to me. I gave it to her and told her how my sons found it while playing.

She was very happy with their honesty and admired their behavior, as this level of candor and integrity was rare at such a young age.

My sons were raised to be honest and understand the concepts of permissible (ḥalāl) and forbidden (ḥarām), even in the smallest details. That is why God instilled in their actions, from a young age, a fear of committing what is forbidden and a desire for God's satisfaction and lawful provision.

Muḥammad al-Jawād's behavior and interaction with me did not change as the days passed. Instead, his affection, tenderness, and care for me increased.

When I entered the kitchen to cook, he would follow me to help so that I wouldn't become tired. I would tell him I did not need assistance and ask him to sit near the fireplace because he felt very cold.

He would look at me sadly and say,

> How can I sit near the fireplace and leave you alone in this extremely cold kitchen?

He would not accept sitting and enjoying comfort and warmth; he would sit beside me and start telling different stories so I would not feel bored.

Muḥammad al-Jawād was the keeper of my secrets and the companion of my days. When he graduated, I lost the tender care of my mother for the second time, but pride outweighed sorrow.

Struggle on the Path of Love

Ḥajjah Ḥawrāʾ ran her fingertips over Muḥammad al-Jawād's face, trying to wake him up so he would not be late for school. She prepared his backpack, placing in it a small water bottle and some money so he could buy food from school when he was on break. Muḥammad al-Jawād went to school with his brother Maḥmūd, and when the school day finished, they went home together.

Meanwhile, Ḥajjah Ḥawrāʾ waited for them so they could sit at the dining table together. It is customary that when children return from school, the mother asks about the events and activities of the day and what they ate. Ḥajjah Ḥawrāʾ asked her sons one by one, and when she reached Muḥammad al-Jawād, she said:

> My child, tell me, was the food you had good?

He said:

> Beloved mother, I took nothing, I gave my friend all the money I had.

She asked,

> But you need food; how did you go without food all these hours?

He said:

> Mother, maybe my friend is more in need than me.

Ḥajjah Ḥawrā' did not get angry; she rejoiced and encouraged him always to support his friends when possible.

> I bear witness, Oh Muḥammad al-Jawād, that you are Jawād; you are generous as your mother called you in this world.

Some children crave what is in the hands of other children without being satisfied, but there are great kids like Muḥammad al-Jawād who do everything they can to make other kids happy. Muḥammad al-Jawād was very generous. He not only gave others what they wanted, but he also gave them more than what they needed.

Every child needs nourishment, but he could live on a small amount of food for many years. From childhood until old age, he remained skinny but was very strong.

He avoided money and greed and paid attention to every detail of his life so as not to hurt anyone.

Ḥajj 'Abbās Ḥijāzī was Muḥammad al-Jawād's father; he was a merchant, which meant that Muḥammad's way of life was comfortable. Muḥammad al-Jawād was able to hide the details of his life from the public eye, and many people were surprised when he was martyred. It did not seem like he was the son of a merchant, whether it was in speech or appearance.

On one occasion, he took a picture of himself that showed a small section of his house, and like most people do, he posted it on social media. It did not take long before one of his friends messaged and said,

> Is this your house? Praise be to God; it is very beautiful.

Muḥammad al-Jawād replied that the house shown in the picture was not his, and he quickly deleted the picture out of consideration for his companion, whose financial condition was not good.

Since that day, he has never taken pictures inside his home out of consideration for those whose means of living were not good.

Muḥammad al-Jawād's supplication was always,

> Oh Lord, I do not want money nor comfort; take away everything from me so that I may reach Your love.

His heart was filled with love; he gave everything for love and a higher divine connection.

As soon as the journey of love began, he was embraced by the presence of his Lord. He could control his instincts, so he gave everything he had.

Zaynab's Guardian

Narrator: Zaynab, the martyr's sister

As the youngest among my siblings, I tended to prefer staying indoors with my mother. Meanwhile, my brothers, Muḥammad al-Jawād and Maḥmūd, gradually began exploring the outside world. It seemed to my parents that they believed the two brothers would be safe together, regardless of the dangerous streets.

They were allowed to explore the neighborhood freely, with the only condition that they had to be home for dinner. Neither my father nor my mother set boundaries on how far they could roam. As long as they met the conditions or requirements, they took advantage of their freedom and liberty. They spent their afternoons exploring dilapidated buildings or talking to our adult neighbors while standing on the street, attracting customers.

I began my academic year at the suburban school while my brothers enrolled in a different institution. I recall one day when I returned home from school exhausted and deeply saddened due to the academic pressure and accumulated and mounting exams. My tears could not hide my fatigue; they flowed down my cheeks as soon as I entered the house. At first glance, my brother Muḥammad al-Jawād rushed to my room in panic, thinking that someone had mistreated me. Sitting beside me, he anxiously asked if someone had harmed me. He was like a father to me, always a pillar of support in times of hardship and sorrow. He remained by my side, embracing me in a comforting hug along with his light-hearted words and jokes.

****

One day, I woke up late for school due to physical and mental exhaustion from the previous day. Hastily dressed, I approached my mother and expressed how distraught and embarrassed I would be in front of the principal, who may scold me in front of everyone. Muḥammad al-Jawād had heard my conversation with my mother as I arrived at the schoolyard. Seeing him there, I walked past the principal, knowing he would somehow reprimand me. Surprisingly, however, the principal allowed me to proceed to class. I looked at Muḥammad al-Jawād with astonishment, then went up to the classroom. At the end of the school day, while boarding the bus home, the driver called me. He informed me that Muḥammad al-Jawād had personally intervened with the principal, requesting leniency and asking him not to reprimand me. Despite losing his temper, Muḥammad al-Jawād managed to restrain himself despite being on the verge of losing his temper.

Muḥammad al-Jawād always exhibited remarkable self-restraint.

Hearing those words made my exhaustion disappear, and I became overjoyed. It was all thanks to my protector and brother, Muḥammad al-Jawād; no one punished me. My brother became the talk of the entire school. I felt the urge to proclaim and say,

> He is my brother, my pride.

The incident spread among my peers; I silently vowed,

> Tell my brother he is my second father, my support in this world, and my ally after God. I love him dearly.

His selflessness and unwavering support not only spared me from punishment but also elevated him to the status of a hero in the eyes of our school community.

Muḥammad al-Jawād was very protective of me and disliked seeing me sad. From his perspective, I was his vigilant younger sister, and he saw me as his spoiled little girl, taking care of me more than anyone else.

Every time he stepped out and returned, he would bring bags filled with an array of food, anticipating my needs without a word from me.

Upon hearing his footsteps in the house, I would always rush to greet him, eager to find out what he has lately got in hand. I felt like he resembled that father who came home with bags in his hands, and I resembled that girl who welcomed her father and took her share of the food from his hand. Sometimes, he would leave the house more than once a day and bring me something each time he returned.

I Am Your Brother, Do Not Despair

Narrator: Maḥmūd, the martyr's brother

The chocolate bar tempted me, so I hurried to the elevator of our building and sat on the floor. I opened my small school bag and took it out. Then I left the building to check on my brother Muḥammad al-Jawād, who was seven years old then, to ensure the school bus arrived. However, I realized my appetite had overcome me. The bus came while I was busy with chocolate. I went to the house to ask my father to drive me to school.

Upon my arrival at school, my brother rushed towards me, his sadness and panic evident. He exclaimed,

> While I was getting on the bus, I thought you were with me. I did not realize you were not with me. I turned the school upside down, looking for you! I thought you were kidnapped...You scared me, brother. You scared me!

Memories are strange. We remember things differently, but you always remember the memories that impact the soul. It is very simple; a person forgets everything but does not forget his memories with his brother.

We are brothers sharing a single soul; we lived one life.

The most important factor that helped us get closer to each other was the closeness of age. Although our personalities are similar, there are points of difference between us. For example, my brother had a rather calm personality, but the teachers scolded me for my mischief.

I remember our parents registered us in a sports club in Brazil, and I do not remember a day that went by without me being punished.

I admired my brother's calm personality, and despite his young age, he had high intelligence and awareness

We used to get into many grapples. He would hit me once, and I would respond with two hits. After a fight that lasted for a few minutes, we would exchange looks and burst out laughing as if nothing had happened. We would hug, and things would be completely normal again.

I know everyone has a heart, but my brother's purity of heart was exceptional. He did not let anyone bother him, nor did I bother him. We both set rules.

The rule was:

> Do not touch my friend, nor my brother, nor my family, or we will attack you like a tsunami.

We spent an interesting childhood together in Brazil. When our family moved to Lebanon, we established our lives anew. We enrolled in school and became more engaged in Lebanese society. However, our treatment of each other did not change; we got closer.

After a few years, Muḥammad al-Jawād suggested that we learn to drive a motorcycle. I agreed and climbed up behind him. He stepped on the motorcycle engine, and we started driving when suddenly, the unexpected happened.

Something fell on the ground. Oh my God! We hit a storefront window. We panicked and did not know what to do. The shopkeeper came out scolding us, praying to God to punish us. We were very sad, were unable to utter a single word, and returned home with pale faces. We did not tell my father what happened out of fear and preferred to tell my mother what happened as soon as she returned from Ḥajj.

Anxiety would not let us sleep that night. The shopkeeper's calls kept echoing in our ears. I sat silently for a few minutes, contemplating what had happened. I looked at Muḥammad al-Jawād. He seemed absorbed in his thoughts, and I knew he was also thinking about what had happened.

We discussed our thoughts and found a solution that satisfied everyone until my mother returned from the pilgrimage.

We decided to deprive ourselves of our school fees and save it daily until we had a suitable amount to present to the shop owner to repair the glass and ask for forgiveness.

That day came, and we went to the man's shop. We offered him the amount we had collected from our school fees.

The man looked at us with a questioning look, then asked us the following question:

Where did you get this money from?

Uncle, we collected it from our school fees so you can fix the windows and forgive us.

He smiled, wiped our heads, and said,

I do not want anything from you; may God forgive you and protect you for your family.

He was pleased with our actions, for few people do that at such a young age.

I looked into my brother's beautiful eyes, shining with joy. He had regained his cheerful face, which he had lost since the accident. Fulfilling his duty brought him comfort and reassurance.

****

This raised a bunch of questions in my head.

Why did he do that?

My goal was to find out why.

To be fair in understanding the incidents, the individual must see the reality of matters directly, not through the witnesses' eyes.

That is why I concluded, after his martyrdom, that we do not see what he sees.

We understood and accepted this.

The matter was related to his strong connection with Abū al-Faḍl ﷺ and his lifestyle, which led him to influence me as well.

What I remember quite vividly is what Muḥammad al-Jawād did on his birthday. That day, we decided to celebrate at home. I went outside with him to buy a gift, but on his birthday, he did not wait to get any gifts; he considered his birthday my birthday.

That day, something unusual happened. He bought me shoes and gave them to me as a gift.

He shared his joy with me. He gave me the shoes and said with a smile on his beautiful face,

> Happy Birthday.

I loved my brother, and I loved his love for me.

I wish they would bury me with him.

I later learned from his friends how much he loved and was attached to me. They told me that in every session they gathered, he used to tell them stories about me. He bought me an ʿAqīq ring;

I still have it to this day. He expressed his love for me in words and actions.

We ran every errand together. He was not good at driving a car, so when he wanted to go to a remote area, he would ask me to give him a ride so we could go together. My companions were his companions. Muḥammad al-Jawād always wanted me to be by his side, but there was a small problem. My brother was very unpredictable when it came to leaving the house. We used to agree with our friends to go out, and my brother would agree, but after a few minutes, he would change his mind. I did not understand what made him act like this, but I think he had a different perspective about going out.

I used to get very upset by him doing this, For I wanted us to share all the good times.

Now, I would love my brother to see my self-reliance and success in life.

He never treated me as if he was older than me, but he always understood more than me. For example, he used to ask me to do some work and take responsibility.

On one occasion, we were going to buy a motorcycle, so he asked me to go with him. When we arrived, he gave me money and asked me to give it to the bike's owner and drive it to the house. He made me take responsibility without realizing it, and I was happy.

My brother raised me to shoulder responsibility and instilled self-confidence despite our close age.

When his comrade, Ḥasan Sallūm, was martyred, he was very sad. But he did not say a word. Their friendship was very strong. On the birthday of his comrade, he brought a cake, engraved his picture on it, and celebrated his birthday with us at home; we all read Sūrat al-Fātiḥah to him. He also hung his pictures on his motorbike because of his strong attachment to him. He asked me to take him to the shrine of the martyr Ḥasan Sallūm, located in the south.

However, due to the remoteness of the area and my busy schedule, I could not take him until we planned a day trip, which was just the two of us, to visit the shrine. Sitting beside it, we began, for the first time, to express how much we loved each other—something we had never done before. I believe that the martyr Ḥasan Sallūm played a role in this moment. Because martyrs are deeply drawn to the Divine Spirit and its grandeur, I am grateful to him for this blessing.

One day, we went with some young people to a restaurant to have lunch together. We had a good time when we went out. They brought us the bill. Muḥammad al-Jawād took it and paid the account. It is customary for the customer to add extra money to the bill as a tip to the waiter. My brother put in twice the account.

I told him:

> Brother, that is too much. Why did you pay double the amount?

He responded,

The waiter is also tired, and we must give him his due.

I took a portion of the money from the waiter and returned it to him, and he got very upset and called me greedy.

Of course, his words were light-hearted, and he joked. Muḥammad al-Jawād was exceedingly generous, even when he ordered food on the phone. When the worker came to deliver the food to the house, he would give him twice the amount. Whenever we went out, he did not care about how many we were or how much it cost; he always took the initiative to pay. We used to always spend time together under his generosity.

One day, my phone rang; I looked up and saw an unfamiliar number. I knew then it was my brother. Every time he came back from the front, he would call me from a phone shop to come and pick him up. I answered the call:

Hello.

My brother said:

Peace be upon you, my dear brother. It is me, Muḥammad; I have returned. Can you come and get me?

I replied,

Thank God for your safety, brother; wait for me; I am coming.

When I got to the place, I saw his bag on the side of the road. I parked next to the phone store.

He ran outside at lightning speed, lifted the bag off the ground, put it on his back, and climbed into the car as if something had happened to him.

I laughed because I knew he did not want anyone to know that he was one of the young resistance fighters who would go to the front. After all, he wanted to maintain sincerity in his work.

It was said amongst the commanders who later were granted martyrdom,

> If a person wants to become a martyr, he must live as a martyr.

My brother proved through all his actions that he was from the caravan of martyrs. His behavior made it apparent that his martyrdom was near.

As the date of his martyrdom approached, his features gradually changed. He became more beautiful, and his speech became much softer. I remember seeing him delete photos from his phone sometime before his martyrdom. I asked him why he did this, and he did not answer.

In the final steps of this journey, he wanted to erase his trace and delete everything related to him to maintain purity and sincerity.

You are pure, my brother, even in your martyrdom.

Then he put his phone on the table and went to another room. I wonder why he made that move. I opened his phone and somehow retrieved all the photos.

Oh, your beauty, my brother, how your eyes shine, and the sweetness of your smile.

Oh, my teacher, my brother, and the sweetheart of my heart.

****

He entered through the kitchen balcony door into my room, walking through the wall without being hurt. I was asleep. I slowly opened my eyes. I saw him standing over my head, smiling at me, and his face shining bright.

He turned his back on me and went. I wanted to catch up with him but woke up at dawn. I wanted to scream. I shouted:

> Oh mother, my brother visited us in this world a little earlier!

I knew then that he was still with us and had not left. The body was gone, but the soul remained.

It is easy for them to kill our youth, but it is difficult to erase them from the heart, especially my brother. I left my heart and laughter with him when I bid him farewell. On the night of our separation, the pain in my heart was strong; I could not sleep, and tears were flowing like rain on my cheeks. I did not bury him in the Garden of the Martyrs, but I buried him in the graveyard of my heart, and this is what gives me patience to bear the pain of separation. I remember he used to tell me when I was young that when I get cut on my body, I should blow on the wound until the pain cools, but my brother, I try again and again, but the wound in my heart does not cool; it bleeds more.

If their killing of innocent people like my brother is considered manhood and victory, then they have betrayed themselves and lost. He did not die with martyrdom; rather, he is immortalized forever. They have weapons, but we have the Prophet Muḥammad ﷺ and his progeny عليهم السلام. We are not defeated, and we will never die. I know that we came to this world to be tested. I am very proud of the title,

Brother of the martyr.

When we bade farewell to him, my mother told us that our pain would go away when he returned with Imām Muḥammad al-Mahdī عجل الله فرجه الشريف. His return will be wonderful. He will return without a bullet in his eye, carrying the banner of victory in his hand and behind Muḥammad al-Mahdī عجل الله فرجه الشريف. I swear by our Lord, he will return.

Sense of Humor

Muḥammad al-Jawād was distinguished for his ability to embody several artistic personalities; he had great potential to imitate the styles of other people's conversations and the tone of their voices funnily. However, sometimes, he switches from the comic frame to portray dramatic scenes. He was also able to master the most beautiful and difficult kinds of art [the art of imitation], which is difficult for anyone to master; only a few people are good at mastering it. In terms of choosing the characters that he imitates and his unique ability to point out the finest details, he was then able to cast it into a critical comic form, portraying the problems of Lebanese society.

The art of imitation is pretty difficult and can only be done by someone embodying a good sense of humor and the ability to imitate many characters in a way that convinces people (or by a person with a sense of humor and who at the same time can imitate many characters in a way that convinces people). Some people who embody this talent have resorted to presenting television programs dealing with funny topics, which is what Muḥammad al-Jawād did. He participated in a social television program, which dealt with the problems of Lebanese society funnily and entertainingly. However, he did not have the opportunity to participate in the program except once. This led him to resort to many people, searching for a second opportunity to enter the field of acting and participate in other TV programs.

Despite his exceptional talent in comic acting and imitation, he could not participate in other television programs due to Lebanese society's indifference to following sharīʿa laws in their programs, except for a few. Muḥammad al-Jawād was strictly committed to following the Divine Laws. The failure of many attempts led to him removing the idea from his head and giving up the search for participating in other programs to preserve his religion.

Muḥammad al-Jawād did not completely give up on his hobby; rather, he gave up on the search for job opportunities in acting. He continued to act in front of his family and friends, impersonating many difficult and imitative personalities. Through his sense of humor and innocent acting, he brought happiness and joy to their hearts and put a smile on their faces.

The Warm Chastity

Blind, they say I cannot see, and if I see what they do not see, I rely on my insight. I observe my surroundings with my truthful imagination.

Zaynab, the sister of Muḥammad al-Jawād, was a kind and sociable figure, attracting her friends to visit her home. Occasionally, when her friends visited, Muḥammad al-Jawād would be at home and open the door as soon as he heard the doorbell sound. When he saw his sister's friends, his face would turn red, and his gaze naturally sought refuge towards the ground. He then left the house quickly, intending to not socialize with them. Perhaps his modesty exceeded that of a maiden who remains in her home.

He was careful not to attend mixed gatherings (i.e., gatherings where non-mahrams from both genders interact). Such gatherings have always been likened to a land of recklessness and behavioral and psychological deviations. This is why his vigilance in this matter was unwavering, and he reinforced it repeatedly.

Modesty was one of his traits, a quality that shielded him from the ugly evils and clothed him with dignity and respect. Muḥammad al-Jawād was akin to a rose, blooming with the fragrance of modesty. When we speak about his modesty, it extends to his interaction with women and all individuals regardless of their gender or age. Modesty was manifested in the words he uttered, his attire, and even his dining etiquette. Above all was his modesty in the presence of God ﷻ.

This modesty made him vigilant in every social gathering and situation, ensuring he did not exhibit bad manners or utter indecent words. He looked after preserving the purity of his reputation.

Our societies today, especially in Lebanon, witness a lot of gender mixing, which often transgresses religious boundaries and ultimately leads to humiliating situations that force us to speak to the opposite genders. Despite these difficulties, Muhammed al-Jawād distances himself from the opposite gender.

The educational institution in which Muhammed al-Jawād completed his studies witnessed many instances of immodest behavior among girls. However, his surroundings untouched his heart, and he pursued his studies normally. His eyes always gazed at the ground so he would not fall into temptation and sin.

On a challenging school day, all the students in the classroom gathered to take an exam. Muḥammad al-Jawād sat in the front row, and a hard-working girl was seated behind him. While the students were immersed in answering the questions, the girl noticed Muḥammad al-Jawād periodically glancing at his paper and, at other times, gazing into the distance. She assumed he could not answer the questions because of his lack of preparation and whispered,

> Muhammed, Muḥammad, Do you need assistance? I can help you if you want.

In response, Muḥammad al-Jawād, without looking towards her, said in a low voice,

> Whoever deceives us is not one of us. Thank you; I do not need assistance.

Perhaps his response surprised the girl, as anyone in his place would have accepted help due to their uncertainty and lack of time. When the time was up, everyone turned in their papers and left class. The girl approached Muḥammad al-Jawād and began conversing about various topics. He offered her advice with the following words:

> You are a good girl. All I want to tell you is that you should not be like the other girls, that is, do not sit with men, and do not say indecent words and phrases that offend your modesty.

Khumaynī, the Grandfather

Narrator: The martyr's relative

Look at Me; I am the grandfather Khumaynī...

The bright sun cast its luminous gaze, painting the earth with a golden hue. The greenery emerged from its haven, embracing the dawn. Given the clear weather and picturesque landscape, we packed our things and went for a family trip to the village house (the martyr's maternal grandparents' house).

After returning to the South from Beirut (Bayrūt), Muḥammad al-Jawād hurried to wash his hands after eating. Because of his young age, which did not exceed nine years, and his short figure, he could not wash his hands in the very tall sink. He brought a small chair to stand on it and reach the water. However, when he finished and attempted to get off the chair, his foot slipped, and he fell, hitting his chin on the ground.

The injury on his face was concealed because of the blood that completely covered it. Rushing to a nearby hospital, we thanked God and His strength as the doctor reassured us of his well-being, labeling it a minor injury. He wiped the blood from Muḥammad's face, and the source of the bleeding became evident. He then patted the wound and put a white medical gauze around it to protect it from germs and inflammation.

Upon our return, the whole family was gathered, awaiting to see Muḥammad. When we entered the house, his cousins and uncles asked:

> Muḥammad, Muḥammad! How are you? Are you well?

He flashed a radiant smile and said:

> I am in the best condition. I have become like grandfather Khumaynī. Look, I now have a white chin, just like grandfather Khumaynī. Call me grandfather Khumaynī.

His words astonished everyone, as he had not even exceeded nine years and had not lived during Āyatullāh Sayyid Khumaynī's ﵀ era. What inspired him to step forward, and what inner wisdom drove this young boy to make such a statement?

Perhaps the early maturity paved the path for Muḥammad to ascend to higher levels. His life was surrounded by integrity and sanctity. So what can we say about Muḥammad, a child whose soul is as clear as the sky and whose heart is as pure as a mirror, distinguished by an abundant share of awareness and perception? He grew up under the care of a father like Ḥajj ʿAbbās and in the lap of a mother like Lady Ḥawrāʾ, both devout and God-fearing individuals. It is clear that Muḥammad al-Jawād, with his talents and innate wisdom, accepted the educational principles of his upbringing and embedded himself in this framework. Most human psychological impressions are of impact, just as his actions, words, movements, and stillness stem from the quality of his nurturing and upbringing, which affected his soul. He was not just an ordinary child but a great secret.

Unconfined Flight

At night, as soon as Muḥammad al-Jawād closed his eyes, he saw himself as an angel, with two wings illuminating the space with light, soaring alongside Prophet ʿĪsā (Jesus) ﷺ. Muḥammad al-Jawād had this dream in his youth, and he narrated it to his mother upon her return from Ḥajj.

God ﷻ had transformed his hands into wings, just as He had done with Abā Faḍl al-ʿAbbās ﷺ. Perhaps this vision stems from the profound influence of Abā al-Faḍl ﷺ on Muḥammad al-Jawād, who took him as a guiding example.

God ﷻ elevated him beyond the material realm from which he was created as he reached the highest peaks and elevations of the spirit.

Muḥammad al-Jawād's acts of worship were not performed out of mere obligations but were the earnest expressions of a true lover. We do not know much about his worship as he was careful not to let anyone know. It is as if he was enraptured in the love of his Beloved, keen on the sincerity of his intention and devotion. He was far from excessive admiration and conceit, and everything we noticed about his worship was coincidental.

For prayer to be accepted and raised alongside the prayer of Imām Muḥammad al-Mahdī ﷺ, it must be performed at the beginning of its time. Upon hearing the call to prayer, Muḥammad al-Jawād would rush to perform ablution, approaching his Beloved most gracefully. Like a shy lover preparing to meet their beloved, he straightened his clothes, performed ablution, and perfumed himself with a pleasant-smelling perfume. He stood to perform his prayer, beginning with takbīrat al-Iḥrām. With closed eyes, he immersed himself in the love of God ﷻ, recognizing that true love was not perceived with the bare eyes but with the heart's gaze. Muḥammad was also attentive to his pronunciation during recitation; whether it be love, drawing, writing, or prayer, they must all flow with tranquility to feel true pleasure. That is why, when you passed him, it was like he was a sugar cube melting in tea due to his unhurried recitation and pleasure.

In the middle of the night, if you passed by the house's kitchen, Muḥammad al-Jawād was often found awake, conversing with his Lord. After confirming that everyone in the house was asleep, he would leave his room and walk towards the kitchen to offer the night prayer. Surely, the darkness of the night was his solace, transforming him into a radiant and captivating figure. He was so beautiful, and his gaze held such charm that, as years passed, his intense beauty made it almost impossible to meet his eyes. His heart and body were completely burned. Muḥammad al-Jawād was a person who, although troubled by his thin body, was satisfied with a small amount of food to empower his worship. Certainly, the fire of love consumed him entirely.

However, the matter does not end here; rather, he performed his acts of worship wherever he went. Even on the battlefield, he worshiped without any shortcomings. In the silence of the night, he would slip away from his resting companions, entering the vast space of the Most Gracious to find a secluded corner away from the sight of others.

Young soldiers would follow him and see him praying the night prayer, which seemed as if he was soaring with closed eyes. Only divine grace in the depth of night could satiate his longing for God ﷻ.

Upon returning from the war front, he appeared with a pale face and a heavy heart. He would bring a small piece of paper and document the reasons for not attaining martyrdom, even though he lived a virtuous life, was careful not to commit sins, and controlled his heart, will, and all parts of his existence. He was not a captive of his body; rather, his body was captive to his unwavering will, aligned with the will of God. He put his entire existence in a state of self-vigilance, and despite that, his delay in obtaining martyrdom made him write in-depth and without restrictions, searching for the reason for his delay in attaining it. His constant self-accountability was a defining trait.

Afterward, he tended the wounds of his loving heart, seeking solitude in his room to converse with his Beloved. He would hold *Mafātīḥ al-Jinān*, his voice emanating, his supplications filling the skies. Upon entering his room, he would resemble a completely melted candle. When he noticed someone approaching, he rushed to hide the book of supplications. His intentions in all acts of worship were sincere. Perhaps what frightened him most in this world was insincerity and arrogance.

He eagerly awaited the arrival of the month of al-Muḥarram to commemorate it and partake in mourning gatherings. As he does every year, he prepares a headband

and black attire, but the al-Muḥarram of 2015 AD (1437 AH) was unlike any other.

During al-Muḥarram of 1437 AH, Ḥajj ʿAbbās, the father of Muḥammad al-Jawād, traveled to ʿIrāq to observe the holy nights near the master of the martyrs; hence, Muḥammad al-Jawād requested a burial shroud from the shrine of Imām al-Ḥusayn ﷷ. That day, Muḥammad al-Jawād sat beside his mother, and after thinking for a moment, he uttered:

> I feel like this is my last ʿĀshūrāʾ with you.

Indeed, it was his last ʿĀshūrāʾ in this world, but he was not shrouded. He courageously met martyrdom and was buried in his military uniform and his pure blood.

He embarked on the path of martyrdom and had no goal other than God ﷻ. He forsook self-love and worldly attachments and transcended the material realm to unite with God. Muḥammad al-Jawād is the man who foretold his departure from this world and passed as a victorious martyr.

The Turbaned Tea

It is a heavenly teapot, its simmering melody echoing the sound of my heart, ablaze with excessive longing and love. In the blink of an eye, the teapot poured its contents into the cup, radiating a luminance that amazed the crowd.

Did you know that drinking tea makes you more joyful if it is with friends? So imagine if it was with the best of companions, the most honest scholars?

I am not exaggerating at all when I speak of the virtues of this small cup of tea. It is no ordinary cup of tea; it is the tea of the Martyred Sayyid; this cup is extraordinary! But what is the connection between Muḥammad al-Jawād and that turbaned cup of tea?

Inside that house brimming with spirituality, a ten-year-old child called Muḥammad al-Jawād sat in that modern-style room. His mother, Ḥajjah Ḥawrāʾ, entered his room saying:

> My son Muḥammad, there is a wedding celebration tonight graced by the presence of [the Martyred] Sayyid. Why don't you get dressed and prepare yourself, then go with your aunt to that celebration?

At the mere mention of the Sayyids' presence, he quickly stood up, put on his attire, and headed toward the living room to accompany his aunt and her husband.

Upon arrival, his aunt's husband asked his eminence, the Sayyid, for a souvenir photo that brought Muḥammad and the Sayyid together. The Sayyid agreed, and he kissed Muḥammad's forehead. Muḥammad was astonished by his prestige, his heart nearly soaring with extreme joy. After a few minutes, the Martyred Sayyid completed the marriage contract for the newlyweds, and blessings were extended to Prophet Muḥammad ﷺ and his family ؑ.

When the sounds of congratulations and ṣalawāt (prayers upon the Holy Prophet ﷺ and his family ؑ) subsided, everyone began exchanging side conversations, accompanied by refreshments and sweets. Then, the golden cup was served to the story's hero, Muḥammad al-Jawād.

The soul of Muḥammad al-Jawād was fond of the tea of his eminence Sayyid Nasrallah. As he poured it into a glass cup, it appeared like a piece of agate poured into a cup of jewels and dissolved like sugar.

He read the depths of this cup of tea in a way that no one else could read. When the celebration ended, he hurried home, eager to narrate the details of his meeting with the Sayyid to his mother. He said:

> Mother, do you know the tea of [the Martyred] Sayyid is the most delicious?

Surely, it is only natural for the mother to ask her son if he has tasted the tea, and the son's response would be yes. However, it is unusual for him to give this response despite his young age:

> I did not even take one sip of that tea, but it is the tea of Sayyid Nasrallah. It is undoubtedly the most delicious tea in existence.

From this, we can discern that every tea bears its unique essence. The mid-day tea of workers has the taste of weariness and hunger, while afternoon tea shared among the family has the taste of stories and cherished memories. As for the tea of his eminence, the Sayyid has a special elegance, awakening the mind of those with the highest of insight. Only the living martyrs and those with great fortune can taste its true flavor. The less insightful and whose hearts lack purity will remain unaware of the delights in his eminence's tea.

A Picture that Lights Up the Darkness

Having several companions of various ages despite your young age is a quality that many people lack.

The humble shop owner next to Muḥammad al-Jawād's house narrates the extent of their attachment to each other despite the age difference between them. While Muḥammad al-Jawād was in his childhood, the shop owner was a mature young man. Muḥammad al-Jawād spent most of his childhood with that dignified man, the owner of the modest store, until that day after the July War (Ḥarb Tammūz) in 2006 when Muḥammad al-Jawād's eyes fell upon a picture hanging on the wall of the shop, radiating spirituality. The picture depicted the martyr ʿImād Jabr, who had joined the ranks of the martyrs during the July War. He fell silent for a moment and then said:

> Oh, my uncle, do you know what? One day, I will become a martyr, and when I am martyred, I want you to place my picture next to the picture of this martyr.

It was as if he was saying,

> I, too, my uncle, will light up this wall. I will meet this martyr. This dream will come true. I will depart to the heavens and receive the badge of martyrdom.

That picture hanging on the wall distinctly captivated Muḥammad al-Jawād. The martyrs have the quality of excelling more than anyone else in the pulsation of their living hearts. Their hearts ignite and capture the signal from the heavens, and they are struck by eternal divine love, then an army of bees of union attacks their souls.

Years passed, and the picture still clung to Muḥammad al-Jawād's conscience. It did not lose its joy in his senses; its value increased in his heart with time. Until his martyrdom in 2016, he adorned the wall with his blessed picture alongside the pictures of the martyrs of the July War.

Thus, without realizing it, the picture of the martyrs has become one of our most cherished images. Looking at it, we can return to joyful moments and the fragrance of memories we hold dear. We can read their blessed stories through their radiant faces by looking at their noble images.

The Sweetness of His Spirit and Soul

Narrator: The martyr's mother

Some people do not think much about burning candles, but when they see them, they pay attention. Imagine a candle burning bright, giving its all to light up the room. That is similar to Muḥammad. He did not ask for anything in return when he helped others. He just did it because he cared.

One night, the phone rang, and one of our neighbors was calling. She asked me to ask Muḥammad al-Jawād to get some food supplies, and before she finished speaking, he hurried to fulfill her request. Muḥammad al-Jawād gave his neighbor the supplies but refused to take a single penny. In a low, timid voice, he muttered,

> We are your servants, Ḥajjah.

The next day, our neighbor came to visit us with a look of dissatisfaction on her face. I was surprised by her condition.

> Oh, Umm Muḥammad, I am very annoyed with your son Muḥammad, and I do not want to talk to him!

I asked,

> Why, my dear, would you be kind enough to tell me what happened between you?

She said:

> Your son brought me things and did not accept to take the money. I am very embarrassed. Could you give Muḥammad this money?

Ḥajjah Ḥawrā' could not help but laugh, her heart swelling with pride and certainty in the purity of her son's heart. It was as if every action he took was a testament to his otherworldly nature, as if he did not quite belong in our ordinary world. He dedicated himself to serving others, facing injustice, and ultimately sacrificing his life. And now, in his martyrdom, he could return to his true home, joining the ranks of those enlightened souls guided by the noble Abū al-Faḍl al-ʿAbbās ﷺ.

Muḥammad al-Jawād was also proactive whenever he encountered his neighbors holding bags; he would insist on carrying them on their behalf.

He did not want anything from this world except to help others and see them happy. So he walked toward the true compass that leads to God ﷻ.

Muḥammad spent his life drawing smiles on the faces of those he knew. Every time he received his monthly salary, he would throw it on the bed in his room. We were surprised by his action and repeatedly asked why he did it. His reply was always the same:

> I do not want anything, neither money nor palaces. I do not need this monthly salary; take it and give it to someone more needy than me.

When he was present at his father's workplace, he often purchased high-quality sweets for the workers working with him in appreciation of their hard work.

He never made them feel inferior; he treated them like he was dealing with himself. He would not accept subjugating them or looking at them with pity. Upon greeting them, he kissed them on the forehead and thanked them for their efforts.

Muḥammad spread love to everyone, old and young alike. For this immense love, he sacrificed everything to make them happy.

People like Muḥammad are companions to martyrdom, and they walked with it as it walked with them. Indeed, martyrdom seeks their testimony; they saved themselves from death and immortalized life forever with their unforgettable memory. Life begins with the martyrs' remembrance, and their remembrance illuminates the souls of people who yearn for them.

These living ones are quicker than angels to rescue us, the dead.

A Visit to Naynawah

Narrator: One of the martyr's friends

When our plane landed at Baghdād Airport during the early days of Dhū al-Ḥijjah, we went directly to the hotel. I was aware that additional Lebanese Ziyārah groups would stay with us inside the hotel and accompany us throughout the visit; However, I was not acquainted with the individuals from these other groups. Upon our arrival, I was very excited to see Muḥammad al-Jawād among those present. While I had seen him several times at the war front, our relationship was not particularly strong.

After exchanging greetings, we went to our respective rooms—Muḥammad al-Jawād sharing with three scholars and myself settling in with two other young men and an elderly man. That night, Muḥammad al-Jawād visited our room, and we exchanged conversations that allowed us to forge a stronger connection. We each began by introducing ourselves, and I learned about their diverse backgrounds—one continuing his education, another of them employed, and a third volunteering for his jihādi work. As the night grew late, Muḥammad al-Jawād excused himself, reminding us of our early start the next day for our visit to the shrine.

A new scholar joined our group the next morning as we gathered in the hotel lobby. Due to a shortage of rooms, one of us had to give up his bed for the newcomer. Without hesitation, Muḥammad al-Jawād offered his bed to the scholar, inviting him to join the room with the scholars. When we heard about Muḥammad al-Jawād's selfless gesture, we asked him to join our room. He agreed and joined us, and we became inseparable, always accompanying each other to different places.

At first, Muḥammad al-Jawād was very shy, but that barrier soon dissolved, and he became close to us. Although we took turns waking each other up for the morning prayer, the young man who led this initiative was Muḥammad al-Jawād.

Amid scorching temperatures of 104°F (40°C) during one of our Ziyārah days, while the sweat was pouring down everyone's face, Muḥammad al-Jawād was afraid that the sun's rays would harm us. He began checking on our conditions and sprinkled water on our faces individually. Due to his selfless actions, he was often mistaken for someone who works within the Ziyārah group, but they did not know he was a visitor like them.

People typically made just one visit to the shrine due to the intense heat. I joined Muḥammad al-Jawād and two other companions at the shrine on a particular occasion. After returning to the hotel, we headed to our room for rest. On the way to our room, we encountered a recently acquainted young man who asked us to accompany him to the shrine as he had not visited the Imām yet. While the rest of us hesitated, as going twice under the scorching rays was difficult, Muḥammad al-Jawād readily agreed. Concerned for his well-being, I advised,

> Muḥammad, you are tired. You should relax so you can visit tomorrow.

He insisted he was not tired and accompanied the young man to the shrine. I do not recall instances where Muḥammad al-Jawād turned down someone's request. He meticulously preserved the dignity of others, even in the smallest details.

Muḥammad al-Jawād embodies the noble virtues represented by Abā al-Faḍl ﷺ. Everyone on this journey noticed his actions when we mentioned thirst or water. He consistently took the initiative to offer water and ask if we were thirsty, always mindful of our well-being.

One day, I was in the room when I casually mentioned my thirst in his presence. Before I could complete my sentence, he gracefully rose from his bed, fetched water, and offered it. At lunchtime, he would prepare our food and ensure each plate was filled. He would only eat once he confirmed we all had enough.

His benevolence transcended these acts of kindness. Muḥammad al-Jawād's delightful sense of humor fostered a deep connection with all of us, young and old. In his absence, a void of boredom and unease permeated our surroundings. This became evident when he accompanied his aunt's husband on a journey to al-Kāẓimiyah, taking them about fifteen hours to get there. Inquiries and concerns about his whereabouts echoed among us,

> Where is Muḥammad al-Jawād? When will he return? He has been gone for a long time. Call him.

I do not know what the secret is in his presence among us. An indescribable sense of comfort and reassurance enveloped our being in his company. A young man of dignity, radiating prestige and beauty, he shielded himself from the pitfalls of sin.

As our stay in ʿIrāq neared its end, we made our way to the shrine to bid our final farewell. At that moment, he turned to me and asked to take a group photo, saying:

> Abū Turāb, let us take a group photo between the two shrines; perhaps you will be destined for martyrdom soon and intercede for us.

Muḥammad was surprised, asking,

> By God, what are you saying? Martyrdom? Me?

I said:

> Muḥammad al-Jawād, all your actions indicate you are a martyr.

Muḥammad denied it, saying

> No, no, someone like me will never attain martyrdom. Perhaps my fate lies in a car accident.

Every time we attributed the title of martyr to him, he denied it and would say he was not worthy of it, saying someone like him does not deserve martyrdom. Yet, if individuals like Muḥammad al-Jawād do not attain martyrdom, what can we say about ourselves, the sinners?

During our Ziyārah, we encountered a Lebanese boy named ʿĪsā, around fourteen years old. Despite their age difference, ʿĪsā's spirit became closely attached to Muḥammad al-Jawād and became very close. We often saw ʿĪsā in the constant company of Muḥammad al-Jawād. One memorable day during our Ziyārah, as we engaged in conversation, ʿĪsā pulled out his phone and began video recording with Muḥammad al-Jawād in the room. With admiration, ʿĪsā introduced Muḥammad al-Jawād as the pure martyr, saying,

> Look at this martyr, the pure martyr.

However, Muḥammad al-Jawād immediately asked him to turn off the camera and replied,

> Stop that, what martyr? I will die in a car accident.

This video circulated on social media after Muḥammad al-Jawād was martyred. ʿĪsā always expressed deep admiration for him with words of respect and appreciation, describing him as a pure and faithful young man. Despite this praise, Muḥammad al-Jawād would humbly express discomfort and say he is just ordinary.

As our visit ended, preparations for our return to Lebanon began. ʿĪsā sought Muḥammad al-Jawād's phone number to stay in touch, and they exchanged contact information.

Muḥammad al-Jawād advised us to persist in reciting Ziyārat ʿĀshūrāʾ and Duʿāʾ Kumayl, emphasizing the importance of not neglecting them. Amidst his conversations, he frequently quoted the sayings of the

Imāms 🕮, especially his grandfather Imām Mūsā al-Kāẓim 🕮, as his family's roots traced back to him. He urged everyone to avoid backbiting.

Upon learning of his martyrdom, though not surprised, I felt a mixture of joy for his attainment of martyrdom and sorrow for his departure. When his pure body arrived at the mosque, I received a call to attend. I witnessed his body on the washing table, his face radiating a heavenly glow, yet one of his eyes had shared in the pain of Abū al-Faḍl🕮. Seated beside him, I wiped his pure head and kissed his forehead. I am unsure what this strange feeling was. I felt extreme comfort in his presence as if I was in the company of a great man greatly cherished by God

Muḥammad al-Jawād was a truly pure, exceptionally rare individual. He devoted himself and his body to the service of others, seeking closeness to God 🕮.

Take the Hand of My Daughter

An elderly gentleman, adorned by the wisdom of age, has experienced enough life's lessons to discern between good and bad. A man like him, whose heart is a sanctuary for the love of Imām al-Ḥusayn ﷺ, how could he not distinguish between noble character and faith and those who are vile and distant from virtue, completely detached from religion? This faithful man encountered Muḥammad al-Jawād on the paths of Karbalāʾ, where the mercy of the master of the martyrs and the tears of those yearning for our martyred Imām ﷺ are found. In Muḥammad al-Jawād, he found a pure young man worthy of marrying his daughter. He found a righteous young man, or as they say, a living martyr capable of taking his daughter's hand towards paradise. Thus, he did not hesitate to offer Muḥammad al-Jawād his daughter in marriage upon their return to Lebanon, willing to give him his heart. For how can one entrust their heart to anyone but the righteous and pure, who truly knows and fears God? Muḥammad al-Jawād found a young man truly deserving of standing among the companions of Imām al-Ḥusayn ﷺ.

Let Your Presence Be Among Us

The martyr's cousin:

When he realized I create photos of martyrs, he asked me to design a special photo for him. Muḥammad al-Jawād rarely liked to ask anyone for anything, and when he was forced to ask for something, you would find him overcome with shyness. On that particular day, Muḥammad asked me to create a photo for him similar to what I designed for the martyrs after their martyrdom. I usually put the martyr's photo in the background and frame it with phrases such as:

> O Qā'im from the Progeny of Muḥammad ﷺ,
>
> Ya Zahra,

or

> Ya Zaynab.

He continued,

> My cousin, would you kindly write next to the photo:
>
> > The Martyr Sayyid Bāqir?
>
> Can you also place the photo next to the Shrine of Sayyidah Zaynab عليها السلام?

I replied:

> I smell the fragrance of martyrdom from you.

As always, whenever someone would associate martyrdom with him, he would bashfully deny it [as if to acknowledge that this status was a high achievement granted by God ﷻ only to His selected few]. He would tell me that he would not reach martyrdom. However, I was certain that this was his destiny. I also felt that deep within his heart, he knew it too.

***

The martyr's friend:

At 1 a.m. one night, I was asked to choose one of the brothers to accompany me on an urgent mission. There were many young men to choose from at the base, including Muḥammad al-Jawād, with whom I had close relationships. I considered everyone and finally decided to ask a young man named Abū Ḥaydar to be at my side. With his agreement, we headed out.

Upon returning, I discovered that Muḥammad al-Jawād was very upset with me and refused to talk since I had not chosen him to accompany me on that mission. His heart would ache, and he would become saddened when he was not selected for a particular assignment. On the contrary, he would consider it a Divine Blessing whenever he was chosen.

Muḥammad al-Jawād had a pure heart and did not hold grudges against anyone. His dedication would see him wanting to be involved in every single mission. He could not stay upset for too long and asked me if I was ever in a similar situation again and had to choose to take someone with me on a mission. I would always choose him to be at my side. And I agreed.

****

The martyr's aunt:

When he learned I would travel to Irān, he hurried to visit me and say goodbye. He hugged me and kissed me on the cheek. I told him that there was a good chance we would have the opportunity to meet Āyatullāh Sayyid Khāmina'ī. His eyes widened, and he smiled. He asked me to send his greetings to our Supreme Leader and to tell him:

> The youth of the Resistance send you special salutations.

He humbly asked me to convey his special greeting to our dear Leader.

He reached into his pocket, took some money, and said,

> Take this, my dear auntie. This is a small amount which I can offer you. Perhaps you might need it during your travels.

I could not accept it and let him know that we had enough money. He refused to take no for an answer, and when he left my home, the money remained at the center of our table.

As soon as he returned from a particular mission, he would turn on his phone and check in on everyone in the family. I never once felt that he was my sister's son; rather, I always saw him as my own—the apple of my eye! My heart bleeds at his mention and his effect on us all.

He would often visit me at work, resulting in the security guards becoming used to his coming and going. Eventually, they all became friends. He would sit with them as if he were one of them, and they would share and discuss their matters. However, he never disclosed any details about his affiliation with the Resistance. What was remarkable is that the security guards also smelled the fragrance of martyrdom from him. They would tell me that his facial features resembled those of our dear martyrs. They even asked to take photos with him so that they would have something to remember him by after his martyrdom.

The Scent of a Father and the Memory of a Son

Narrator: The martyr's father

The aroma of nostalgia fills my senses, mingling with memories of a beloved son.

My heart raced, beat by beat as if thudding against the walls of my chest. My son had been away for a long time, and his prolonged silence only heightened my concerns. I was unaware of his whereabouts, and when he would return, so I hastily sought out an official knowledgeable about his situation to calm my heart. Fortunately, things went well.

At last, Muḥammad al-Jawād's voice breaks through the silence after an eternity of anticipation. Yet, his words did not offer the reassurance I craved. Expressing annoyance at my call, he stated,

> I prefer not to talk with you right now nor in this situation. None of my friends have reached out to their families yet. I see no reason to be an exception, Dad.

After returning exhausted from his service at the war front, he would not immediately seek rest; instead, he would leave the house to check on his friends and see how they were doing, often returning late. When questioned about the reason for his tardiness, he would explain that he was in the company of elderly individuals and could not leave them. He felt too polite to do so. He patiently waited for them to leave before returning home, exemplifying his respect for elders.

Furthermore, he would dedicate time to assist me at my workplace on his vacation days. I recall when a young man gave him 100,000 L.L. (Lebanese Līrah), asking to exchange it. After exchanging it, the young man wanted to tease him, so he claimed he was short 20,000 L.L. Muḥammad al-Jawād retrieved 20,000 L.L. from his pocket, insisting the young man take it. Even when the man assured it was a joke, Muḥammad al-Jawād insisted,

> So that nothing remains on my conscience.

As the end of each month approached, I would inquire,

> Muḥammad, do you have enough money?

He would respond,

> Yes, Father, praise be to God.

Yes, Muḥammad al-Jawād had money, but how much? A mere thousand Lebanese pounds is barely enough to buy a tissue. Whenever he received his monthly salary, he would help his friends who were newly married or had children and could not cover their expenses. He was not satisfied with giving them a little but rather all the money he had.

I always offered to get him married and buy him a house so he would enjoy a comfortable life; however, he insisted on wanting nothing for himself, urging me to give everything to his brother, Maḥmūd. Not once did he ask for anything for himself; even during travels for work, when I reached out to the family and asked them for their needs, everyone would request something except for Muḥammad al-Jawād. He never requested anything for himself. Naturally, I would not return empty-handed; I would always bring him something special. Sometimes, I would bring clothes that did not fit him well. But he would graciously accept them, as silence is a testament to his humility and respect for my efforts.

Oh, my dear son! You are unwavering support and selflessness with all your actions, and you never failed to uplift me. This was not merely during adulthood but ever since he was young. We spent some time together at my brother's house, the house of Muḥammad al-Jawād's uncle. Muḥammad al-Jawād was about ten years old. That day, his cousin accidentally shut the door on his [Muḥammad al-Jawād's] delicate hand, causing it to bleed. Muḥammad al-Jawād almost lost consciousness from the severity of the pain. Yet, even with the intensity of his suffering and pain, Muḥammad al-Jawād's concern was not for his well-being; rather, he tried to shield his cousin from blame.

> I am the one who closed the door on my hand without meaning to. My cousin did nothing wrong. I hurt myself.

This is how my son spent his life—influential, victorious, and a martyr.

Blind Is the Eye That Does Not See You

Narrator: The martyr's father

The bill has been paid, my uncle...

Initially, I took my wife, my daughter Zaynab, and my son Maḥmūd on a trip southward. Muḥammad al-Jawād was not with us as he was at the war front. Upon arrival, we stopped to eat savory pastries at a bakery called Abū 'Abbās, famous for its delicious bites.

After entering and enjoying some pastries, we made our way out to pay the bill. Outside, I asked the cashier:

> As-salāmu 'alaykum (peace be upon you), how much is the bill?

He said,

> The bill has been paid, my uncle.

Ḥajj 'Abbās insisted,

> Sorry, but I have not paid yet. There must be a mistake.

The cashier explained,

> No mistake, sir. The gentleman who greeted you upon your arrival took care of your bill.

My wife and I shared a look of bewilderment. We had not greeted anyone that day or encountered anyone familiar.

Is it not strange? I had not greeted anyone.

Dear reader, let us delve into this incident together. Surely, what happened must be connected to the family of Prophet Muḥammad ﷺ and his descendants عليهم السلام. Perhaps the family of martyr Muḥammad al-Jawād received special care from Ahl al-Bayt عليهم السلام. Indeed, the Imām عليه السلام sees us, and we do not see him. While the Imām عليه السلام knows us individually, it is unlikely he greets everyone. While he knows us one by one, does he greet us all? Of course not. Blessed is the one whom the Master of our Time, Imām Muḥammad al-Mahdī عجل الله تعالى فرجه الشريف greets.

Peace Be Upon My Uncle ʿAbbās

Narrator: One of the martyr's friends

One fateful night, the perilous proximity of enemy forces rendered the young men's food delivery impossible.

One night, the young men were unable to deliver food to us due to the proximity to enemy forces, so one of us had to take the initiative to go and bring food. Muḥammad al-Jawād went with a friend from our group to bring food. When they returned, they placed the food on the ground in front of the brothers, then Muḥammad al-Jawād brought the bowls and began pouring food for everyone, one by one, and when he reached his bowl, the food was completely gone. One of the young men approached him and asked Muḥammad al-Jawād for his share, but he refused and said he did not like this food and would prepare something else for himself. We already finished all the food, but we thought he had found something to eat. A young man among us went to wash his bowl and saw Muḥammad al-Jawād sitting in the corner with a piece of old, crusty bread, eating it secretly, out of everyone's sight. The young man's heart was broken to see Muḥammad al-Jawād in that state without anyone knowing. Then the young man came and told us what he saw.

Usually, there were about twenty personnel in the center, including those who guarded its perimeter day and night.

Our duties were carefully allocated among us, with some tasked with guarding throughout the night while others kept watch during the day. It was understood that no individual could shoulder the burden of day and night shifts simultaneously, recognizing the immense toll such a responsibility would exact on anyone's endurance.

One night, Muḥammad al-Jawād's turn was to distribute the night guard shifts. Many of us would object when it was our turn to guard at night due to the time and the fear of being unable to perform the night and dawn prayers. But Muḥammad al-Jawād never objected and guarded with complete satisfaction and pleasure. That night, everyone slept, and the next morning, we saw Muḥammad al-Jawād still in his place on guard duty.

As we convened to assign guard duties amongst ourselves, Muḥammad al-Jawād, without a hint of complaint, took up the mantle of the night shift. It was a duty often met with reluctance by many due to the late hour and the apprehension of missing the pre-dawn prayers. Yet, Muḥammad al-Jawād, unwavering in his commitment, stood guard with unwavering dedication. The night passed in tranquility, and as dawn broke, we were surprised to find Muḥammad still at his post.

We were all astonished and wondered who should be guarding instead of him. One of the young men came forward and told us that it was his turn, so we asked him then:

Did you guard?

He said,

> No, I did not.

We asked,

> Why?

And the brother explained,

> The brother who finishes his shift is supposed to wake up the next brother to take the shift for him, but Muḥammad al-Jawād did not wake me up.

Everyone began to wonder who guarded after Muḥammad al-Jawād. Everyone said they did not guard during the night. We knew then that Muḥammad al-Jawād carried out the guard alone and did not want to wake anyone. He also purposefully chose to guard at night instead, a duty no one else wanted, so the young men could enjoy a good night's sleep while he stood guard.

Role Models

Narrator: One of the martyr's friends

That day was marked as one of the harshest days of the relentless summer heat, as we were in Ramaḍān. I was sent with Muḥammad al-Jawād to Idlib (Syria) with some brothers. The takfīrīs were not far from our location. As night fell, We were instructed to remain on high alert, knowing that the enemy would launch an attack at any time soon. We stood firm and patient, but some remained anxious and in suspense. Muḥammad al-Jawād was by my side. His mere presence was a source of solace, his words a balm for my troubled mind. He would joke and laugh with everyone as if there would be no attack on us soon. He was brave and was never afraid. After that night, things became more complicated, and clashes with the enemy intensified. Lives were lost, and martyrs were made.

Several days later, on the first day of 'Īd al-Fiṭr, the young men began calling their families and greeting them. It was my turn. I ended the conversation and offered Muḥammad al-Jawād to contact his parents, but he refused. I was surprised by his behavior and did not understand the purpose of this action. His soul was very attached to his parents, especially his mother, but he refused to contact them despite that. Days passed, and the incident was still stuck in my head. I later found out why he refused. He did not agree to contact his parents because he believed that speaking from the public treasury was a violation.

It was strictly for orders and duty, for charity, not something he had a right over, and he believed it was not permissible.

Each of his attributes indicated the sweetness of his soul and the approaching time of his martyrdom. We always joked with him that he was one of the martyrs of 1982, as they were the best men and martyrs.[7]

After several days, we were permitted to visit our families. That day, a young man revealed his financial hardship to Muḥammad al-Jawād and some of his brothers. The brother had not even finished his speech yet when Muḥammad al-Jawād put his hand in his pocket and gave him everything he had. The young man asked him if he had more money to return to his house. He said he still had money to return home, so the young man thanked him and left. Muḥammad al-Jawād did not have his phone to call his family to bring him home, and he did not have any money left for a taxi.

He had no choice but to walk home from St. Michael Church to his home in Ḥāret Ḥreik[8] (around a 20——to 30-minute walk). He did this to help his companion endure hardships for those he loves and to make others comfortable.

Everyone who saw Muḥammad al-Jawād was certain he would be the first among us to be martyred.

---

[7] Referring to the resistance group who were martyred in 1982.

[8] A mixed Shīʿah and Maronite Christian municipality, in the Ḍāḥiyah suburbs, south of Beirut, Lebanon.

The Righteous Servant

Narrator: One of the martyr's friends

After a while, Muḥammad al-Jawād and I were sent with many brothers on a mission to the countryside of Qunayṭrah (in Syria), where we stayed there for a long time. Despite the cold weather and falling snow, Muḥammad al-Jawād's great humor relieved our fatigue. As we were divided into groups to accommodate the rooms, not all of them had heaters. Some of us sat in extremely cold rooms, while others enjoyed the warmth in warmer rooms. Muḥammad al-Jawād and some young men were divided into a room with heating. He opposed staying in the room and swapped places with one of the young men in a room without any heater, even though he would get colder than everyone else and his face would change color. To comfort the young men feeling cold, he did something funny to entertain us—he brought all his clothes and wore them, appearing like a giant man. Thus, he turned the scene from fatigue and bitter cold into a scene full of laughter and joy. I do not know where he would come up with these entertaining actions; it was all to make us feel as if he was not affected by the cold and to ensure that he did not take the place of any young man enjoying the warmth.

That day, there were Syrian forces in the rooms adjacent to us. One approached us, asking for a visit to get to know everyone. We agreed, and I, along with Muḥammad al-Jawād and another young man, went with them. As soon as I walked in, I instantly noticed the cups in front of them, which contained ʿarak, an alcoholic beverage, and they asked us to drink with them without specifying what was in the cups. I realized they contained ʿarak, but Muḥammad al-Jawād did not notice. I could not bring myself in front of them and tell him not to drink, but I was also afraid he would accept their invitation as he did not like to refuse anyone's request. I thought of a way to convey to him not to drink, so I came up with the idea of using gestures. I began talking to the Syrians, telling them that we try to engage in these actions solely to seek the satisfaction of God ﷻ, then quickly glanced at Muḥammad al-Jawād. At that moment, he understood what I meant and declined to drink. After we left the room, he thanked me for preventing him from drinking. I told him we have to protect and warn each other when necessary. I looked at him and noticed his complexion had changed; he fell silent and began holding himself accountable for a sin he had not committed.

The next day, we were sitting and watching an episode of the Irānian series called *al-Mukhtār ath-Thaqafī*, specifically the episode where Kiyān is martyred. I looked at Muḥammad al-Jawād and saw him deeply moved. He was on the verge of bursting into tears but restricted himself from crying in front of us.

Meanwhile, one of the young men came and said,

> We need to gather in the other room as the food has arrived.

The meal was small and barely enough to fill our hunger. Muḥammad al-Jawād would eat half of his meal, which would not even feed a small child, and give the other half to one of us. He would say he was full and could not finish the other half. This continued throughout our stay there, and whenever he finished eating before everyone else, he would sit in the corner of the room until we finished eating. When we finished, he would gather all the dishes and head to the kitchen to wash them. Despite our refusal, he insisted, saying,

> Let me wash them; what honor is greater than serving the mujāhidīn.

Sometimes, I would wake up in the middle of the night to find him standing in the kitchen and washing dishes with cold water in the winter, his sweet smile and radiant face accompanying him. I always felt and still do feel humble in the face of his selfless actions.

Muḥammad al-Jawād had a slender body, yet he endured hardship and fatigue more than us. He always prepared tea and would not drink until he ensured everyone had a cup. Sometimes, when there was not enough left for him, he would say he did not want tea but coffee, all in consideration of our comfort and to avoid causing us any embarrassment.

Please Wipe Your Hand on My Head, My Master

Narrator: One of the martyr's friends

One night, I sat with the youth division and Muḥammad al-Jawād in one of the training camps in Wādī al-Biqāʿ (Beqaa Valley). The camp consisted of several rooms, about thirty meters apart. Muḥammad al-Jawād sat on the ground next to several other companions, chatting. Meanwhile, I was on the bed, watching them. In the corner of the room, a young man was reciting the Noble Qur'ān in a beautiful voice. As for the others, some were sleeping, some were chatting, and others were lost in thought. Muḥammad al-Jawād and three young men sat with the brother, reciting the Qur'ān. When he finished reciting the Noble Qur'ān, he closed it and put it aside. Then he went up to his bed to lie down.

Meanwhile, I felt that something blocked my hearing in the place that we were in, and I could no longer hear what the young men were saying. A beautiful, majestic man appeared before me with an enlightening face and an aura of light. He approached Muḥammad al-Jawād and stroked his hand on Muḥammad al-Jawād's head. Then he stroked the heads of the young men with Muḥammad al-Jawād. Afterward, he went toward the sleeping men and stroked his hand on their heads. He entered the remaining rooms before heading outside. No one saw him. I followed him outside and asked him who he was, and he told me;

“I am Ṣāḥib al-Zamān عجل الله تعالى فرجه الشريف [Imām Muḥammad al-Mahdī عجل الله تعالى فرجه الشريف]. I work nearby in the Qalamūn region, so I passed by to wipe your heads."

That year, the battle in Qalamūn was fierce, and the takfīrīs had recently entered the area. After the encounter with Ṣāḥib al-Zamān عجل الله تعالى فرجه الشريف and recalling his words, I tried to follow him, but I could not catch up; he was walking very fast as if the ground beneath his noble feet was collapsing.

I gathered the youth division together, with tears running down my face. I told them what had happened. Everyone started crying, and loud noise filled the room. Some of them were crying, and some of them were beating their faces. The next day, they sent us the battalion commander, and he requested that I retell the story for everyone. The Commander understood the message and said:

> Ṣāḥib al-Zamān عجل الله تعالى فرجه الشريف blessed the soldiers by wiping their heads and, therefore, guiding their steps.

With the passing of days and months, a group of the mujāhidīn whom Ṣāḥib al-Zamān عجل الله تعالى فرجه الشريف had wiped on their heads became martyred, and Muḥammad al-Jawād was amongst them. As for the rest, they are sincere and God-willing; they will continue on the path of martyrdom.

The Devoted Servant

Narrator: One of the martyr's friends

Muḥammad al-Jawād always kept an eye on everyone's business, both on the front lines and off. He carried around a little notebook everywhere, jotting down every little thing. If he borrowed money or something, he would note it down, scared he might forget to pay people back.

He was really serious about whatever he did, especially when it came to praying. Even in cold and snow, he would step out of his shelter to pray in the dark. When we asked him what he was up to at night, he would say he was hungry and went out to eat.

When it came to his work and responsibilities, he was all in. Sometimes, he would wear his helmet even when there was no danger around to show he was serious about his duty to God. We cannot praise Muḥammad al-Jawād enough for his sincerity and dedication.

I remember one time we all decided to tease him to see how he would react. We started saying disrespectful things about the resistance to get a rise out of him. But we realized we had gone too far when he got really mad. He asked us not to joke about that again. His love for the resistance and its leaders was deep and unwavering.

The next day, our neighbor came to visit us, looking dissatisfied. I was surprised by her condition, and we had a nice conversation.

> Oh, Umm Muḥammad, I am very annoyed with your son Muḥammad, and I do not want to talk to him!

Muḥammad al-Jawād's mother replied,

> Why, my dear, would you be kind enough to tell me what happened between you?

The neighbor replied,

> Your son brought me things and did not accept to take the money. I am very embarrassed. Could you give Muḥammad this money?

Muḥammad's mum laughed at that time and became more certain of how pure her son's heart was, as if he was proving in all his actions that he did not belong to this world of ours. He came to serve the people and was wronged, so he was killed and could return to his first home with that enlightened Master called Abū al-Faḍl al-ʿAbbās ﷺ.

You Are the Forerunners, and We Are the Ones to Follow

انتم السابقون ونحن اللاحقون

Narrator: One of the martyr's friends

Muḥammad al-Jawād got to know the martyr Ḥasan Sallūm on the battlefield.

They had been very attached, and their friendship was more than mere brotherhood.

Muḥammad al Jawād's heart always yearned for his friend Ḥasan as they would always be seen together, yet we did not know much about their personalities, and what can we know? They are both martyrs.

Ḥasan attained martyrdom on August 2, 2015, when he was only 17 years old.

His friend's departure saddened Muḥammad al-Jawād, and he constantly talked about him until, after five months, he too attained martyrdom to join his friend!

Muḥammad al-Jawād forged a deep connection with Martyr Ḥasan Saloom amidst the chaos of the battlefield. Their camaraderie surpassed mere brotherhood, evolving into an unbreakable bond that defined their existence.

While always seen together, the enigma of their personalities remained shrouded in the veil of martyrdom. Their journey was one of selflessness, as both Muḥammad al-Jawād and Ḥasan Saloom ultimately embraced the path of sacrifice and valor.

Ḥasan Saloom, who was only seventeen, met his martyrdom on August 2, 2015, in the town of Zabadāni. The departure of his dear friend weighed heavily on Muḥammad al-Jawād, transforming his demeanor. His every word echoed with memories of Ḥasan, a testament to the profound impact of their friendship.

Unable to bear the void left by Ḥasan's absence, Muḥammad al-Jawād joined the noble ranks of martyrdom after a mere five months. Their intertwined destinies serve as a poignant reminder of the sacrifices made on the battlefield and the enduring spirit of comradeship that transcends the limitations of mortal existence.

I am Departing, My Friend

Narrator: The martyr's friend

He said to me:

> My brother, the heart of a martyr senses when the time of his martyrdom is near, do you know? But my heart remains silent.

A week before the martyrdom of Muḥammad al-Jawād, he called me to bid farewell before heading to the war front. He informed me of his departure to the front and mentioned that I was one of his closest friends. I told him he was also a friend and brother dear to my heart. He continued by saying:

> My brother, the heart of a martyr senses when the time of his martyrdom is near, do you know? But my heart remains silent.

I felt as if he was bidding me farewell and telling me that the time of his martyrdom was near. I sensed he had become someone different from the Muḥammad al-Jawād I had previously known. His condition had improved. I asked him why he expressed those words, and his response was:

> Nothing, my brother. I advise you to look after all the youth and friends, take care of them, and send them my greetings individually.

He listed their names, remembering everyone. At the end of our conversation, I asked him which area he was heading to, to which he replied,

> To Idlib in Syria.

The situation was very dire in Idlib at the time, with extremist groups still present.

They truly know the time of their departure, my friend; the heart of the martyr is his guide.

The Consoler

Narrator: One of the martyr's friends

We activated the warrior spirit, and Muḥammad al-Jawād and I stood ready to enter the countryside of Idlib, as requested by the Riḍwān Brigade.

Upon reaching the area, bullets began to pour over us like raindrops. Dust filled the region, and we could not settle in one specific place. I could easily recognize the voice of Muḥammad al-Jawād among the sounds of gunfire.

We had no choice but to crawl through the mud. The mud's thickness was approximately 30 cm, forcing us to crawl.

After extensive effort, we reached a point where we could settle in. Upon arrival, Muḥammad al-Jawād opened his bag to eat his breakfast. He had a bit of mortadella and some chocolate. He was about to eat his sandwich when he looked at me and felt my hunger without me uttering a word. He handed me the sandwich, saying he was not hungry. His selflessness mirrored that great man who delivered water and refused to drink without his family. He said,

> Here, eat breakfast and enjoy this chocolate.

After five minutes, the takfīrī terrorists started shooting again, mortar shells from here and sniper shots from there. My main thought during those tense times was the well-being of Muḥammad al-Jawād. I turned towards him to check on him, but what I saw broke my heart and deepened my sorrow. I saw a young man whose face was entirely covered in light, a radiant face with a majestic appearance, a sharp gaze, though his dark eyes were lost into the vastness of the most Merciful. His beard was long, the sun hitting it with its bright rays. He was my candle that night, and I remembered my uncle 'Abbās for how much he resembled my dear uncle, peace be upon them both. He was calm and reassured as if we were not in a situation of attack and confrontation. I had never seen him like this before. I told him:

> You may leave us tonight, my beloved, and join the ranks of the martyrs.

He replied:

> Will God ﷻ accept someone like me?

We tried to communicate with others via a wireless radio device, but we could not. The radio signal was lost, and we were no longer in contact with the other teams. We thought for a moment about what we should do. Sayyid Bāqir (Muḥammad al-Jawād) got another radio to secure communication between the team leader and other teams. I did not accept, and we discussed who should go under the bombing and bring a radio, but to no avail. Muḥammad al-Jawād refused to let me go and said that he was the one who must go. There was not enough time to discuss this further; I could not stop him, and one of us had to go immediately.

Muḥammad al-Jawād left the position with the light accompanying him. Due to his condition, I became more worried about him, feeling that he may not return except as a martyr, but I kept hoping for his return.

A quarter of an hour passed, and Bāqir did not return. I did not know what I should do. After five minutes, I heard the sound of gunfire towards our position, and I became more worried about him.

A long time passed, and he has not returned. I had to do something. Meanwhile, a team arrived to help. I asked them to give me a radio to communicate with the other divisions and check on Bāqir to see if he had reached them. At first, I communicated with the Riḍwān Brigade, and they said Bāqir had not arrived yet. I still had hope that he had reached the Mujtabā Brigade. I contacted them, and they told me he had not arrived.

I could not leave the place and search for him because of my duty at the brigade. At that moment, I asked a young man near me to go and see where he was; I asked him to check on Sayyid Bāqir. He went, and my heart began to beat intensely.

Time passed, and the young man returned with a pale face, saying:

> Abū ʿAbbās, congratulations to Sayyid Bāqir on what he has attained; He has joined the ranks of the martyrs.

I looked around the area as if I could see heavy gunfire and rising dust in a dream. I felt suffocated and could no longer stay there. I could not feel my feet anymore. I burst into tears, but what flowed from the eyes was not water, but rather a soul dissolving and dripping. I remembered his state just a few hours ago. I felt sorrowful in that place and returned in a state worthy of lamentation.

We retrieved his body with immense difficulty. The weather was very cold, and the mud prevented us from moving how we wanted. The cursed enemy did not stop firing at us, which caused our movements to halt. We had no choice but to wait until darkness fell to enter the area and retrieve his pure body. We arrived and saw him, what a sight! Alone on the battlefield, without washing or shrouding, one of his eyes was consoled by his dear uncle ʿAbbās; peace be upon him. The injury was in his eyes. The enemy used bullets that exploded inside the body upon entering; as soon as the bullet hit the pure eye of Sayyid Bāqir, it exploded inside his head, leading to him joining the ranks of the martyrs.

The Best of Stories, Part Two

Narrator: The martyr's mother

> You will live,

I was told.

> You will live, and immortality will be written for you. You have a lofty position with God.

I asked,

> How can I live when I am alive?

They told me,

> You will attain what you have longed for all these years, and you will live and be resurrected.

When the religious scholars of Irān and Lebanon heard about this dream, many interpreted it. At first, they could only say,

> Is there such a living being among us? This is not a human; it is a pure angel.

Then, they all agreed on one interpretation: Muḥammad al-Jawād has an extremely elevated status with God, which no one else can attain. As for the turban he saw, it symbolizes his leadership. When the Martyred Sayyid gave it to him, it indicated support and his imminent departure from the world through martyrdom.

And this is what happened after Muḥammad al-Jawād had this dream for twenty days. He ascended as a victorious martyr, realizing his dream as he always used to say,

> Victory, victory, and then martyrdom.

Farewell, O Martyr of God

Narrated by the Martyr's Mother

On January 31, 2016, I watched on television during the news bulletin that an explosion had occurred in Syria. My world turned upside down because I knew that Muḥammad al-Jawād and his companions stayed in Syria for one day before heading to Idlib. I remained silent and said,

> May it be for the best, God-willing.

I do not know why I felt so unsettled that day. Since I woke up and left the house, I had forgotten several things and had to go back repeatedly. My day was far from normal. And when I heard the news, I became even more scattered.

As I was sitting, my phone rang, and I answered. My cousin asked me to meet him downstairs in front of our building. When I arrived and greeted him, I saw sadness in his eyes, and he did not seem well. I got into his car, and inside was one of the scholars I was acquainted with. I greeted them, and they asked me about myself. It was then that I sensed and suppressed the feeling that my son, Muḥammad al-Jawād, had been martyred. I looked into their eyes and asked,

> Did Muḥammad become a martyr?

Then I asked if he had been martyred in the morning's explosion. At that moment, I wished for him to have attained martyrdom on the battlefield rather than in some explosion.

When I confirmed his martyrdom on the battlefield, I whispered,

> I longed to embrace him to my chest, how I wish he would return, and bid him farewell.

As for his mother's condition, I will leave the word to her:

I was sitting at home when Ḥajj ʿAbbās approached and informed me that his cousin had called him, asking him to come down from the house because he was waiting for him inside the building. I asked my husband to come to our house instead of standing outside the building. He said he wanted to speak to him; perhaps he wanted something, and then he left.

Moments later, the doorbell rang, and it was my neighbor, the woman. I later learned that Ḥajj ʿAbbās had asked them to come to our house and inform them about the news of Muḥammad al-Jawād's martyrdom and asked them to inform me. I opened the door and welcomed them. I saw tears welling up in one of their eyes, and I thought she was sick. I said to her,

> You must be ill.

It never occurred to me that my son had been martyred. After they entered, they asked me to wear my cloak so that their husbands could come and have tea with my husband.

My son Maḥmūd was still asleep. When he woke up, he came to me and told me that his companions had been calling him continuously, and his phone would not stop ringing. He asked me the reason for that. At that moment, I told him I had no idea what his companions wanted from him.

Just before I put on my cloak, one of them received a phone call, and my son Maḥmūd heard her say:

> Now we will tell her that Muḥammad al-Jawād has been wounded.

Then he came and told me. Here, I began to connect everything: my husband's cousin, my neighbors, my son's companions, and Muḥammad al-Jawād's injury.

I hurriedly ran to the living room and told them,

> Muḥammad has been martyred.

They insisted that Muḥammad al-Jawād was injured, not martyred, but I told them,

> No, Muḥammad has been martyred.

I sat for a moment in my room, feeling like I was going to burst out of my skin from the intensity of distress and confusion. Tears streaming down my cheeks, I whispered,

> O Pure One, O Muḥammad, O Believer, O Muḥammad."

Of course, at that moment, my daughter Zaynab was deeply saddened by the loss of her brother, to whom she was somewhat attached. As for my son Maḥmūd, I can say here that he lost not only a brother but also his companion, support, and soul. His backbone was shattered.

Muḥammad al-Jawād's body was at the military complex. When a mother is on her way to see her son's body, life momentarily stops. When we arrived, I saw his face had turned into a halo of light. He remained as he was, beautiful, but one of his eyes had been injured, and so consoled by his uncle ʿAbbāss b. ʿAlī ﷺ.

Martyrs, some are like Imām al-Ḥusayn ﷺ, who have their heads cut off, and others, like ʿAbbās, who endure several wounds. Thus, the flames of love warm their hearts.

In the morning, his body was still at the al-ʿAskarī complex when a young man came to us, someone we did not know beforehand. He told us that he had seen a man whose face radiated with light the previous night in his dream. He climbed onto the Abi al-Faḍl al-ʿAbbās ﷺ dome, lowered the flag, and handed it to him. He asked him to go to the complex and give them the flag to be lowered with Muḥammad al-Jawād in the shrine. Upon waking up, he brought the flag of Abā al-Faḍl al-ʿAbbās ﷺ, which he had kept before, from the dome of ʿAbbās ﷺ and gave it to us. And so we wrapped Muḥammad al-Jawād with it.

A few months after his martyrdom, he came to one of the sisters I knew beforehand in the dream, and she asked him about his status in Paradise. He told her then that his neighbor was Abū al-Faḍl ﷺ. Many people have seen many visions, one of which is that the maqām (station) of ʿAbbās is built above his grave.

> When a person dies, their earthly endeavors end, and they depart from the worldly abode. However, the scenario takes a different turn for a martyr and martyrdom. As a martyr ascends, their physical body perishes, yet their soul endures and exerts an even more potent influence.

Since Muḥammad al-Jawād's martyrdom and until today, I have never felt that he is absent. When I speak to him, he hears me and sees me, and I see him.

One day, I waited for everyone in the house to sleep to arrange the living room for the condolence (majlis) gathering that would be held in my house early in the morning. To save time, I decided to arrange the living room at night. When I finished, I looked at his picture on the wall and spoke to him. I do notam try to remember if I asked him to attend the gathering with us or if I asked him if he would attend tomorrow, then I went to sleep.

In the early morning, my husband, Ḥajj ʿAbbās, told me that he saw Muḥammad al-Jawād the previous night, sitting on the couch in the living room under his picture, wearing his home clothes as if he had returned from work, tired, and embraced us, smelling our scent. Then he quietly ascended to his picture hanging on the wall. I smiled and was very happy, so I told him what had happened the previous night.

There are also two similar incidents in which Muḥammad al-Jawād appeared to us while we were awake.

It was the last day of the blessed month of Ramaḍān, and Maḥmūd was still asleep. Zaynab and Ḥajj ʿAbbās had gone to fetch some items and had not returned yet. Meanwhile, the call to the maghrib prayer was made, so I went to pray. During the prayer, I heard a door opening, thinking Maḥmūd had woken up. After a while, Ḥajj ʿAbbās and Zaynab came. I heard Ḥajj ʿAbbās asking Maḥmūd to wake up for breakfast. That is when I realized that something had happened that I did not know how to finish my prayer. I did not know what I was reciting anymore. When I finished, I asked Maḥmūd if he had woken up a while ago and entered the restroom. He said,

> No, he never woke up, and his father just woke him up now.

The second incident occurred a day after his birthday. On his birthday, I visited him at the Shrine of the Martyrs, told him that I had brought a cake to celebrate, and asked him to attend.

The next morning, I was still sitting on the bed, browsing my phone. I saw someone pass by my room door at lightning speed, and I could not determine who it was. I thought it might be Ḥajj ʿAbbās, so I entered the living room looking for him but could not find him. I went out to the house balcony, and he was sitting there. I asked him if he had entered the house and walked past our room, and he said he had not.

People thought that my son had been killed and erased from this world. You were mistaken. He has become even more present. I ask him to attend, and he always comes. But I remember that one day when I spoke to him, he had been absent for a long time. I told him I missed him and asked him to come, and he answered me through his father.

He came to me in the form of his father. He saw me standing, performing prayers in the place where I always pray at home. Muḥammad al-Jawād hugged me, and Ḥajj ʿAbbās said to him:

> Do you only hug your mother?

So he approached and hugged his father as well. I asked him in the dream why he had not come to visit me, and he replied:

> Mother, I am busy with a session with the Imām of our time عجّل الله تعالى فرجه الشريف.

This dream occurred on the day commemorating Imām Muḥammad al-Mahdī's عجّل الله تعالى فرجه الشريف apppointment as the final Imām.

The Last Thing I Remember...

Narrator: The martyr's mother

When Muḥammad is mentioned, the thread of memories entwines around the heart endlessly, bringing forth memories.

That day was among the last of Muḥammad's memories, his final visit to his aunt's house. The night dominated the atmosphere, and Muḥammad alone illuminated all those present like stars in the night sky.

His aunt's husband confirmed this to us after his martyrdom. On that evening, as we gathered, he swore that as soon as we entered, he felt as if I were the mother of a martyr, my husband the father of a martyr, and Muḥammad al-Jawād was the martyr.

He would gaze at Muḥammad remarkably, his eyes overflowing with love and admiration for his luminous face.

On that day, Muḥammad remained silent and smiled continuously. My brother-in-law refrained from requesting a photo together, fearing I might see them and sense the nearing of Muḥammad's martyrdom.

Upon returning home, I was struck by the scene of Muḥammad bidding farewell to his aunt, whom he embraced with overwhelming love, as he was headed to his jihādī work in Syria. I said to him:

> Do you love your aunts this much?

He laughed,

> I love them because they are my aunts, and I also love them because they are your sisters, mother.

The last farewell moments after Muḥammad's martyrdom were heavy, yet that day felt lighter than a breeze because we were accustomed to saying goodbye to Muḥammad.

When the early morning arrived, we prepared to bid him farewell, and I handed him the bags. It was customary for his father to remain asleep, as he would bid him farewell in the evening. However, that day, he woke up early and bid farewell to us.

Our embraces were the highlight of the moment.

Muḥammad approached the elevator, then turned towards us with his tearful eyes that overwhelmingly gazed at us.

All those painful details were not felt during the last farewell; they passed in a normal, mild manner. But when we received the news, we remembered those moments in detail. All signs indicated that he would attain martyrdom —his appearance, embrace, face, eyes, and the last hand gesture he made.

Yes, he bid us farewell physically, but his spirit remains with us and never leaves us.

The Beloved of al-ʿAbbās

When Muḥammad al-Jawād was martyred, Umm (mother of) Fāṭimah, the daughter of the martyr's neighbor, was still pregnant with her daughter. She dreamt of Muḥammad al-Jawād shortly before giving birth. In her dream, she saw the doors of both her family's house and Muḥammad al-Jawāds's house, which were directly opposite each other, wide open, with no barrier in between.

Muḥammad al-Jawād, dressed in white, graced her with a soulful smile while holding her daughter, who appeared as if her age was one and whom she would name Fāṭimah upon her birth. She heard Muḥammad al-Jawād tell her daughter:

> Send my greetings to your family.

Umm Fāṭimah was terrified when she saw this, thinking he would soon take her daughter to him. Days passed, and she gave birth to Fāṭimah. A year later, Fāṭimah, now one year old, appeared to her mother just as she had been in her dream before her birth.

A profound secret exists between Fāṭimah and Muḥammad al-Jawād, yet we do not know what it is. Inside their building's elevator is a picture of Muḥammad, and as soon as Fāṭimah sees this picture, she looks at it strangely, embracing the image as if she already knew him.

Fāṭimah also told her mother about an incident that happened some time ago. She had embraced a picture of

Muḥammad al-Jawād and fell asleep. When she woke up, she told her mother about her dream:

> I saw martyr Muḥammad, with Lady Ruqayyah عليها السلام leading the way, and him following her path. They came to me, Oh mother.

What could be the secret between Muḥammad al-Jawād and Fāṭimah?!

A Turning Point

Narrator: The martyr's sister-in-law

Many stories are filled with lessons. The hero of these lessons may be a person or a situation; this story of mine is the best proof.

Firstly, I was born into a family that feared God ﷻ but was not religiously committed. When I was young, I did not know anything about the teachings of the Islāmic religion. All my parents taught me was that God ﷻ sees us everywhere, and we must feel His presence. In addition to that, I learned to respect all people, whether old or young.

Years passed, and I began studying at the Lebanese University in Beirut. I met many students, most of whom were from the Shīʿī sect. One of my peers often talked about Islāmic law, so I began researching and understanding the Noble Qur'ān more. People told me I was modest but without a scarf.

I had mutual friends with the martyr Muḥammad al-Jawād, but I did not know Muḥammad al-Jawād personally. I remember texting a friend one day, asking him how he was doing. He sent me a picture of himself on a walk along with Muḥammad al-Jawād and his brother Maḥmūd. It was the first time I saw Muḥammad al-Jawād. Days passed, and social media was flooded with pictures of the martyr Muḥammad al-Jawād. I asked my friend who is the martyr. He told me that he was that young man in the picture he last sent me. I was despondent and said,

May God have mercy on him.

I went to sleep and saw Martyr Muḥammad al-Jawād in my dream. Muḥammad al-Jawād was sitting in the last seat on the bus, and the bus was crowded with young men. I was not sure who they were. As for me, I was sitting in the second seat. Suddenly, Muḥammad al-Jawād quickly sat in the front seat and shouted,

The bus will be bombed! Pay attention, everyone!

Indeed, the bus got bombed, and a fragment pierced his pure shoulder. The bus halted; the young men then carried Muḥammad al-Jawād and took him off the bus, chanting,

Ya Zahrā', Ya Zahrā'.

The next day, Muḥammad al-Jawād was buried in Rawḍat al-Ḥawrā' (a burial place for the martyrs of the holy defense, found in Beirut, Lebanon). A few days later, I was there with my friends. I recited Sūrat al-Fātiḥah at his tomb, then went and sat at the tomb of the martyr 'Abbās Samahā and began reciting the Qur'ān. Martyr Muḥammad al-Jawād did not have his tomb on the grave yet.

From that day on, I began to go to the Rawḍat frequently and visit his tomb.

One day, specifically a Friday night, I went to visit him. It was the first time I heard Du'ā' Kumayl, as many visitors were grouped reciting the Du'ā', which changed my life completely. I sat next to the grave of Muḥammad al-Jawād and began doing the same. And so, every Thursday, we went to the graveyard.

Months passed, and I got to know the martyr's family better. My relationship with them grew stronger. The martyr's brother admired me, and I also admired him and his good morals. We started planning our engagement, which was scheduled for after Muḥammad al-Jawād's martyrdom anniversary.

Martyr Muḥammad al-Jawād's birth anniversary came by.

I needed clarification about what to gift him for his birthday. I could not find a gift as great as the gift of putting on the hijab. I wore the hijab and went to the martyr's house to accompany them to the graveyard. Ḥajjah Ḥawrā' opened the door and asked me to come in. She did not say anything about my hijab. I then entered the house, which was crowded with women. I sat next to one of them, and she said,

> Congratulations on wearing the hijab.

I thanked her.

Ḥajjah Ḥawrā' was surprised

> Have you committed to the hijab? I thought you only wore the hijab when you went to Rawḍat al-Shahīdayn!

She then approached and kissed me on the head. When the martyr's brother—who later became my husband—learned about this, he was very happy.

Today, my life and how I have changed were greatly influenced by Muḥammad al-Jawād's martyrdom. As part of the martyr's family, I can see the dignity of the martyr day by day.

I am always moved by the stories I hear from his mother.

Indeed, when we lose our way, we must call upon the martyrs to take our hand toward the love of God ﷻ and the path of piety, faith, and loyalty.

Tawāf in the Ḥaram

The Qur'ān depicts various colors and images of the confrontation between truth and falsehood and how the people of truth, with their faith and patience, triumphed over the strongest leaders of the devil's party and their followers. The contented women and the sacrificing warriors are at the forefront of these noble people of truth.

Ḥajjah Ḥawrā' al-Riz is among those who devoted their lives to serving Islām; a pious woman who wore the garments of chastity and modesty, surrounded by an aura of prestige and dignity, as she combined courage and faith. She is a model of educational motherhood who exerted great effort towards her son. She taught him the concepts of Islām, instilled in him a love for the good of mankind, and encouraged him towards jihād and martyrdom in the path of God ﷻ. He drew inspiration from the faith of his mother, who raised an educational banner with which she gained precedence in the role of the Muslim mother.

Muḥammad al-Jawād was deeply attached to his mother from a young age in a noticeable way. His affection towards her did not diminish as the years passed; it grew stronger. He did not spare any gathering he attended without speaking about her and expressing his love for her, whether at work, within the family, or anywhere else. This is evident in his famous saying:

> No one loves us like our mother; she is the only princess in my blood, heart, and soul.

He made her his princess and mirrored her in her character, appearance, and logic.

His devotion to his mother existed not only before and after his martyrdom but also during and after it. He always promised her to stay by her side, and he fulfilled that promise.

It had only been a few weeks since his martyrdom, and his sister Zaynab's friend saw him in a very special dream.

Zaynab was sitting with her friend, and Ḥajjah Ḥawrā' was beside the grave of Muḥammad al-Jawād. Suddenly, a light emerges from his grave, and Ḥajjah Ḥawrā' turns her gaze towards that light and speaks to it; then Muḥammad al-Jawād approaches her and puts his hand on her shoulder, asking her to be patient and promising to meet her upon the blessed reappearance.

After that, the years passed. Ḥajjah Ḥawrā' goes to the grave of Muḥammad al-Jawād alone. Meanwhile, she receives a voice message on her phone. She opens it and discovers a message from one of the neighbors of Muḥammad al-Jawād's grandfather [from his father's side]. The woman says she had seen Muḥammad al-Jawād in her dream, and they were together on a Ziyārah [visit] to 'Irāq. Upon hearing this, Ḥajjah Hawra smiled and addressed him humorously and kindly:

> Are you visiting 'Irāq with the neighbor of your grandfather's house and not taking your mother who raised you with you?

The visit ended, and she returned home. Three days later, her phone rang, and the caller was a sister from among the sisters. She tells her that the previous night, she had dreamt of the shrine of the Master of the Martyrs, Imām al-Ḥusayn ﷵ, and it was a sight full of beauty. As for the number of people inside the holy shrine, it was very few. She saw her [Ḥajjah Hawra] and Muḥammad al-Jawād circling the shrine of the Master of the Martyrs together.

The dream's interpretation revolves around Ḥajjah Ḥawrā's request from Muḥammad al-Jawād to accompany her to the holy shrine.

This pious and righteous man resembled his mother in character and appearance. Whenever you miss him, look at his mother's face.

My Dear Polite Teacher

Narrator: The martyr's teacher

Dear Muḥammad, I have always thought I was your teacher until you surpassed me, and you became my teacher; you taught me that this world is too lowly for us to exert ourselves in seeking it. My beloved, kind, polite, and exemplary teacher, I trust your promise. My heart has begun to detest this world and sees it as that prison you liberated from. You are alive with your Lord; pray for my release from captivity.

—A teacher of Muḥammad al-Jawād at the school institute, mourning him upon his testimony.

****

My dear, polite teacher

Dear Muḥammad, I have always thought I was your teacher until you surpassed me and became my teacher. You taught me that this world is too low for us to strive for. My beloved, kind, polite, and exemplary teacher, I trust your promise. My heart has begun to detest this world and sees it as that prison you liberated from. You are alive with your Lord. Pray for my release from captivity.

—The teacher of Martyr Muḥammad al-Jawād at the school institute, mourning his rise.

The Gate of Wishes

﴿وَلَا تَحۡسَبَنَّ ٱلَّذِينَ قُتِلُواْ فِي سَبِيلِ ٱللَّهِ أَمۡوَٰتَۢا
بَلۡ أَحۡيَآءٌ عِندَ رَبِّهِمۡ يُرۡزَقُونَ﴾

﴾*wa-lā taḥsabanna lladhīna qutilū fī sabīli llāhi 'amwātan bal 'aḥyā'un 'inda rabbihim yurzaqūn*[a]﴿

﴾*Do not suppose those who were slain in the way of God to be dead; no, they are living and provided for near their Lord*﴿[9]

If martyrs were to remain in the worldly realm, they would have fulfilled the needs of those who ask to the extent possible. But now, they have departed this world, and God has made them alive, as He said in His noble book, "*they are living*," negating the attribute of being dead from them.

Just as Ahl al-Bayt ﷺ has taught us to deal with the martyrs as if they were alive.

Go to the graves of the martyrs and greet them with 'As-salāmu 'alaykum,' addressing them fully just as you would address those who are alive. They will hear you and see you because they are connected to the Master of the Martyrs ﷺ, and they are his children. God ﷻ has extended their hands; they have fulfilled their duty. How can we benefit from them? Do not close this door; enter it. They hear you, see you, and follow up on your affairs. This is how they are because they are connected to the Master of the Martyrs ﷺ.

---

[9] Sūrat Āl 'Imrān, Verse 169.

Many people have sought intercession through Muḥammad al-Jawād to fulfill their needs, and they were fulfilled by the grace of God 🕮 and the martyr. We will mention some of them.

One of the sisters:

I am not religiously committed, and I do not have a strong connection with the Ahl al-Bayt 🕮 and the martyrs.

I had a dream about Sayyidah Fāṭimah al-Zahrā' 🕮. I asked someone to interpret the dream, and it meant that I would meet a Sayyid. I did not think much of it until one of my friends asked me to accompany her to Rawḍat al-Shahīdayn (where martyrs are buried in Beirut) without prior knowledge of my dream. I went with her to Rawḍat al-Shahīdayn. When I entered, it was as if someone was guiding me on a path. I walked in a certain direction until I reached one of the martyrs' graves. I glanced at the grave and read the name written on it: Sayyid Muḥammad al-Jawād Ḥijāzī. At that moment, I realized the meaning of my dream. I sat beside the grave and decided to open the Noble Qur'ān and dedicate some verses to him. It is worth mentioning here that I have never completed the Noble Qur'ān in my life, and I do not know the names of all the chapters. I opened the Noble Qur'ān, and Sūrat al-Qamar appeared before me. It was the first time I knew that there was a chapter in the Noble Qur'ān called al-Qamar. I read the chapter and dedicated it to him. I told myself that I should get to know more about the biography of Imām Muḥammad al-Jawād ﷺ, after whom the martyr Muḥammad al-Jawād was named. As the days passed, someone gave me a Ḥirz from the shrine of Imām al-Jawād ﷺ. Of course, it was not an ordinary coincidence but a secret connected to the martyr Muḥammad al-Jawād. Since my first visit to the grave of martyr Muḥammad al-Jawād and learning about his life, my religious commitment has improved greatly. I always visit him and recite Sūrat al-Qamar; I ask him for my needs, which are all fulfilled.

Ḥajjah Sanā' and her intercession through the martyr:

Ḥajjah Sanā' has a young son suffering from autism. She tried many times to enroll him in a plethora of schools but could not succeed as schools refused to admit him because of his illness, which he was not at fault for. Some schools accepted him but demanded unreasonably high fees.

After various failed attempts, Ḥajjah Sanā' found herself present one day near the Imām al-Qā'im mosque in the southern suburb of Beirut. She saw a picture of the martyr Muḥammad al-Jawād hanging on the wall, mourning him with it and calling for the funeral procession of his pure body. Her heart yearned for his sweet smile and pure face, but she was unable to participate in his funeral.

After several months, she was informed by someone from a school near Rawḍat al-Shahīdayn. She took her son's files and spoke with the school's principal. As usual, her son was rejected this time as well, but this time, her heart was overwhelmed with pain and sadness. After leaving the school, she went to Rawḍat al-Shahīdayn and sat near the grave of Muḥammad al-Jawād, bursting into tears. She sought intercession through him and swore on him by his forefathers ﷺ and Imām Mūsā al-Kāẓim ﷺ. She asked him to help her with her son's issue, then left, holding back her tears.

Two days later, her phone rang. One of her friends asked her to take her son to a specific school. She gave her the address and said that transportation was the only fee she needed to pay the school.

But it did not end here, for Muḥammad al-Jawād is kind and generous. He not only fulfilled this need but rather gave her more.

Ḥajjah Sanā''s son cannot speak. He expresses his needs through crying. One day, Ḥajjah Sanā' went to attend a majlis for Lady Ruqayyah ﷺ at the house of the martyr Muḥammad al-Jawād during the days of al-Muḥarram.

After a while, her Ziyārah to 'Irāq for the Arba'īn pilgrimage was facilitated by someone, as she could not afford the cost of the visit. During her visit to Arba'īn, her phone rang, and her daughter told her that her brother, who suffers from autism, called her by her name for the first time. Years have passed, and the boy and his whole life have improved greatly.

> Ḥajjah Sanā' has full confidence in the martyrs, and she always turns to Muḥammad al-Jawād to facilitate her needs by the grace of God ﷻ and through him.

One of them narrates:

> At first, I bought an airplane ticket. I packed my suitcase and prepared for my flight, which took off in two days. This incident occurred in 2020. I contacted the airport in the county where I live, and they told me I am unable to travel without undergoing the coronavirus test called PCR. I tried to contact hospitals and ask them to allow me to come and take the test, but they responded that they could not give me an appointment due to the high demand caused by the pandemic, and I had to wait for several days. I lost hope in traveling and felt very upset about the disruption of the work I would do after arriving. I entered my room, and my gaze fell on a picture of Muḥammad al-Jawād. I stood in front of the picture and began to speak to him with the following words:
>
>> As-salāmu 'alaykum, Muḥammad, how are you? I have repeatedly heard about people seeking your intercession and having their needs fulfilled. Will you respond to me this time? No, no, I am certain that you will fulfill my need; I know that. Do you not see my condition and my discomfort? Do not leave me disappointed.
>
> I then went to sleep. The next day, I went out to go to the store. Upon arriving, I saw a bus next to the store. I

approached the bus and asked them what they were doing, and they told me that they were offering coronavirus tests. I was very happy. I took the test and then asked them when the result would come out, and they told me that it would take at least three days due to the high demand for people taking this test. I was hopeless! The next day, they sent me a text message saying that the result had returned and was negative, for which I was grateful.

Yes, Muḥammad al-Jawād did not disappoint me; he helped me and facilitated my travel with God's help.

An incident related to the son of martyr Muḥammad al-Jawād's father's friend:

The young man found out that he was infected with the coronavirus, and his health deteriorated. The father of the young man asked the father of martyr Muḥammad al-Jawād to pray for his son's recovery at the grave of Muḥammad al-Jawād and ask him for help. The father of the martyr went to the grave of Muḥammad al-Jawād and said to him:

> I want a miracle from you, my son. This is the son of my friend Mūsā, whom you loved very much throughout your life. Now, he is infected with the coronavirus, and his condition is not well. I ask you to improve Mūsā's condition.

Then, the martyr Muḥammad's father went to work. His phone rang, and his friend asked him if he had prayed for Mūsā at the martyr's grave. He replied that he had gone there early in the morning and prayed for Mūsā. His friend laughed and said,

> Mūsā's sense of smell has returned, and he has begun to improve since early morning.

The sister-in-law of the martyr's aunt:

> After forty days have passed since his martyrdom, Muḥammad al-Jawād's aunt' sister-in-law narrates a dream she had with him. He comes to her and says that on such and such day, it will mark forty days since his martyrdom, and he requests her to come.
>
> To confirm the dream, the woman called Muḥammad al-Jawād's aunt and asked her when the fortieth day after his martyrdom would be. She told her it would be on such and such a day, the same day Muḥammad al-Jawād had informed her in the dream.

A believing sister:

> This sister participates in every funeral procession for the martyrs; she never misses any procession. However, because of some circumstances, she could not participate in the funeral of martyr Muḥammad al-Jawād. He came to her in a dream, admonishing her and saying that she had participated in the martyrs' funeral processions. However, she did not participate in his funeral procession, and he asked her about the reason for that.

Yes, he is still alive. He feels and sees and will be saddened if we do not participate in the things that concern him.

After this dream, she went to the martyr's grave, asked for forgiveness, and got to know him better.

The martyr's uncle:

The martyr's uncle was infected with coronavirus. His condition became worse to some extent, which led him to be admitted into the intensive care unit and the use of an oxygen machine to help him breathe properly. After two days, there was no sign of improvement or recovery.

With a heavy heart, he addressed his nephew, the martyr Muḥammad al-Jawād, at noon:

> My dear Muḥammad, I initially did not ask for anything from you, but it has been two days, and my condition is getting worse. I am addressing you now and asking for help; perhaps my condition will improve, and I will recover.

At night, the doctor came to check on him, and his condition suspiciously improved as if nothing had happened to him. The doctor left and informed the nurse that this man's condition had improved significantly. The nurse was surprised and said it was strange, as it was difficult for him to recover quickly. After that, he was discharged from the intensive care unit to a room inside the hospital and later to his home.

The Will of the Martyr

In the Name of God, the Beneficent, the Merciful

In the name of the Lord of the Martyrs.

O God, send blessings to Muḥammad and the Household of Muḥammad and hasten their return.

Peace be upon you, O my Master, O Messenger of God.

Peace be upon you, O my Master, O Commander of the Haithful and Master of Deputies.

Peace be upon you, O my Master, O Sayyidah Fāṭimah al-Zahrā'.

Peace be upon the two Imāms, al-Ḥasan and al-al-Ḥusayn, the masters of the youth of Paradise.

Peace be upon you, O my Master, O Zaynab al-Ḥawrā'.

Peace be upon you, O my Master, O Ṣāḥib al-Zamān.

May our souls be sacrificed in your service, and may the mercy and blessings of God be upon you.

Peace be upon [the leaders of the Islāmic Revolution] Āyatullāh Sayyid Rūḥullāh Khumaynī ﵀, and Āyatullāh Sayyid 'Alī Ḥusaynī Khāmina'ī (may God ﷻ preserve him).

Peace be upon the leaders of the Islāmic resistance, those who have laid the foundations with their steadfastness, vision, and sacrifices, and whose legacy continues to inspire. May God be pleased with them.

Peace be upon the martyrs of the Islāmic resistance,

Peace be upon the honored commander, the guardian of blood, our Master and beloved, His Eminence as-Sayyid ash-Shahīd.

Peace be upon the mujāhidīn in the way of God, peace be upon the wounded in the way of God, and peace be upon you, O pure martyrs.

Peace be upon your souls and pure blood with which victory was achieved.

My beloved mother,

It is beautiful to remain in your warm embrace and your precious affection, but the longing to join the caravan of love, the caravan of Imām al-Ḥusayn عليه السلام, is profound. On the day of my martyrdom, rejoice and be happy, for martyrdom is not death but rebirth. O mother, seek solace in Sayyidah Fāṭimah al-Zahrāʾ عليها السلام and remember the patience of Lady Zaynab عليها السلام on the land of Karbalāʾ. I thank you, my beloved, for all your hard work and effort for me, and no matter how much I thank you and strive with my actions, I cannot do justice to your right, my beloved.

My dear father,

Your discussions taught me a lot: always to trust God first, then myself. Thank you for all your kind words from your kind mouth, and thank you for all your hard work and effort for me, my father. No matter how much I repeat thanks, I will not do you justice.

My beloved brother and sister,

I advise you to remain steadfast on the path of Islāmic resistance, to preserve this path, and to maintain the will of Sayyid ʿAbbās.

Peace be upon you, O my Master and leader, O Abā ʿAbdillāh al-Ḥusayn. Peace be upon you and upon the souls which were annihilated with you. Peace of God be upon all of you from me forever as long as I am existent and as long as there are day and night. May God not cause this [visit] to be the last of my visit to you [all]. Peace be upon al-Ḥusayn, and ʿAlī b. al-Ḥusayn, and upon the sons of al-Ḥusayn, and the companions of al-Ḥusayn. Peace be upon Zaynab al-Ḥawrāʾ. Peace be upon Abū Faḍl al-ʿAbbās, and may the mercy and blessings of God be upon you [all].

The humble servant to the mercy of God ﷻ, Muḥammad al-Jawād ʿAbbās Ḥijāzī, "Sayyid Bāqir".

His sayings

- Resistance without obligation is like prayer without ablution.

- I want to be martyred and in Paradise, but I do not want palaces or beautiful maidens (Ḥūr al-ʿayn). I want a small room, as long as it is near Ahl al-Bayt ﷺ.

- Martyrdom is not death but life.

- My Master, O Abā ʿAbdillāh, even if we were to melt and dissolve, everything we do would be insignificant before you.

- O Imām al-Ḥusayn ﷺ, even if we were to be cut into pieces, this gift (sacrifice) remains insignificant. Everything we do is insignificant before you, my Master, insignificant before your feet.

- The upcoming ʿĀshūrāʾ, I may not be with you.

- We have gatherings on many nights but differ from family gatherings.

- No one loves us like our mother. She is the only princess in my blood, heart, and soul.

- Grant me pure martyrdom, in which I choose myself so that it may be an atonement for my sin.

- The martyr may be absent, O mother, but he does not die.

❖ None of us know the taste of honey; what we eat is not honey. No one knows the taste of honey except those who joined Abā ʿAbdillāh Imām al-Ḥusayn ﷺ.

—Sayyid Bāqir

Declarations About Him After His Martyrdom

Since Childhood

The love of al-Ḥusayn ignited the fire within the hearts

And Dhū al-Fiqār rose high above the chests

How can I find the path to you, my Master guide me.

The childhood dream of a destination in martyrdom

From a young age, embracing the path of guardianship

An illuminating light, a servant of the pure

O Bāqir, to the call you have responded

To meet your Lord eagerly, you have fulfilled

Muḥammad, to the sanctuary, you have become a servant

Muḥammad, to Ahl al-Bayt, a warrior and supporter

Jawād, purity emanated from you like a fragrant scent

Jawād, a thousand swords in Karbalāʾ were purified

Words by: Maryam Qubaysī

****

The bird sang for peace

And the clouds rain from longing

O the beat of my heart, enamored

Through love, you adorned the realm

With the smile of the lips that captivated the skies

With the season of joy crowned with generosity

Smiling are the stars, with love, with kisses

Engulfed by the light on the edge of dawn

Flowers in full bloom, watered with my tears

Muḥammad, a hero, refused to surrender.

On the path of the lovers, the scent of jasmine wafted

In the company of the martyrs

With the glow of the candles

The flocks of birds escorted you to Paradise

And the flowers emanated for you the best of fragrance

Indeed, the fragrance of martyrdom in the painting of joys

And everyone supplicates for the hastening of the reappearance...

Words by: Sayyid Muḥammad Ṭarḥīnī

****

Recite with me from the verse of triumph

Farewell to a martyr with a joyful smile

Send off Jawād, who left us with a gleam

Spread the coffin shroud with flowers in grace

Scatter roses, a tribute to Bāqir's grandeur

Rejoice upon the echo of tragedies reaching

And welcome Muḥammad, the one who departed

He responded to the call of al-Ḥusayn, then parted

You ascended to the heavens, separating from us

You are gone, Muḥammad, leaving behind lost hearts

After your martyrdom, in confusion

Lost in the love of Bāqir, wandering

Longing to meet you, dreaming

Farewell, O Sayyid Bāqir, the light of our eyes

I sacrificed myself and my mother.

So do not weep from sorrow.

And patience from you, in pain and anguish

I sacrificed myself for the covenant

Every part of this covenant for al-Mahdī

Arise and inherent from me after me

To preserve the path and this promise

Words by: Āyah Ḥamadī

Photos of the Martyr

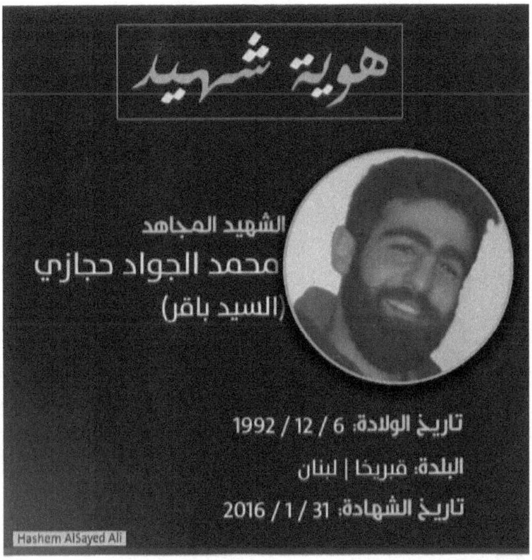

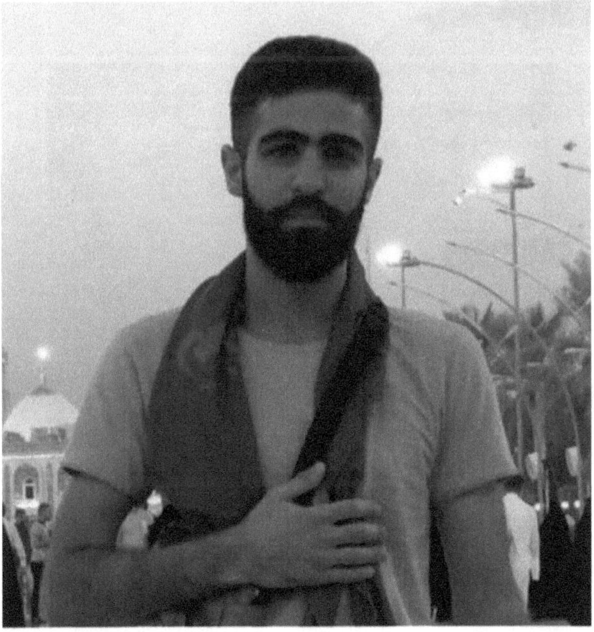

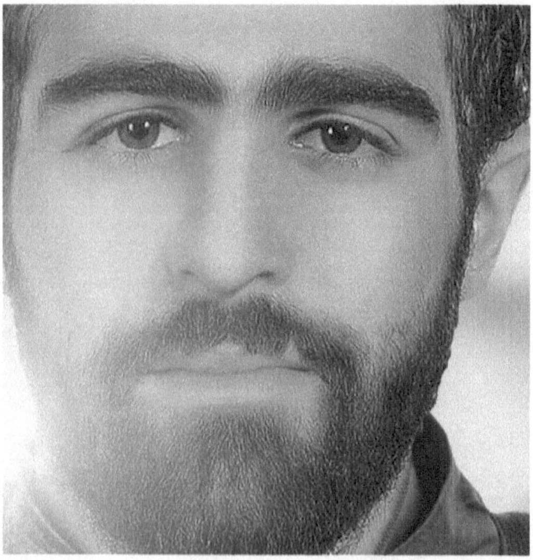

Kha
Zahraa

الشهيد_سيد_باقر

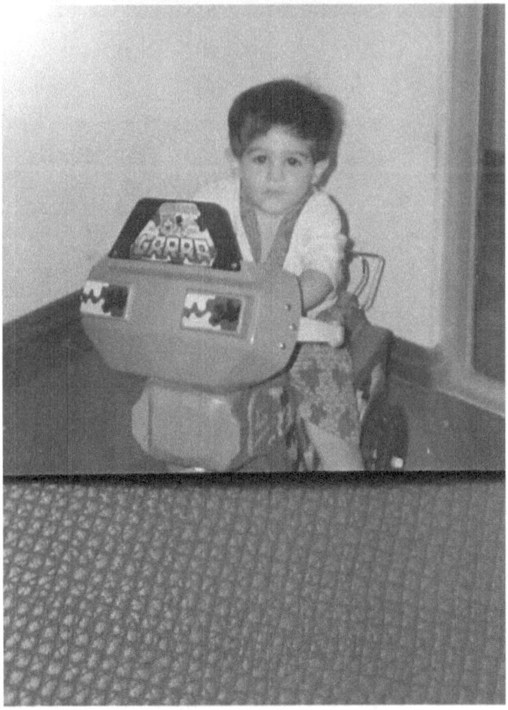

وجزاهم بما صبروا جنة وحريرا
www.facebook.com/Smile.Martyr
صفحة بسمة شهيد

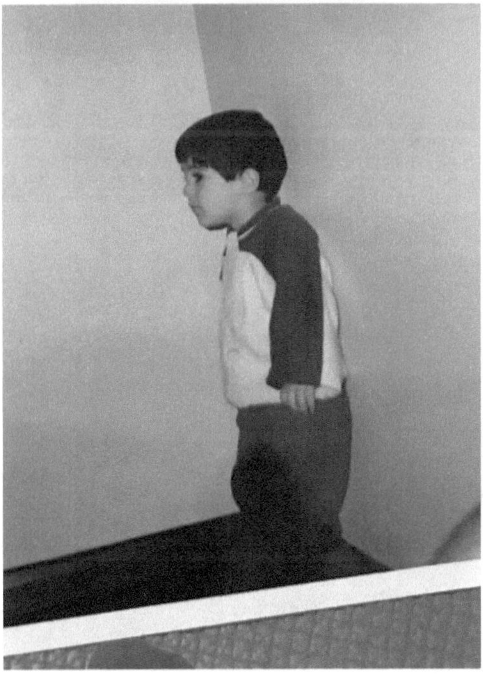

FINE WEAR

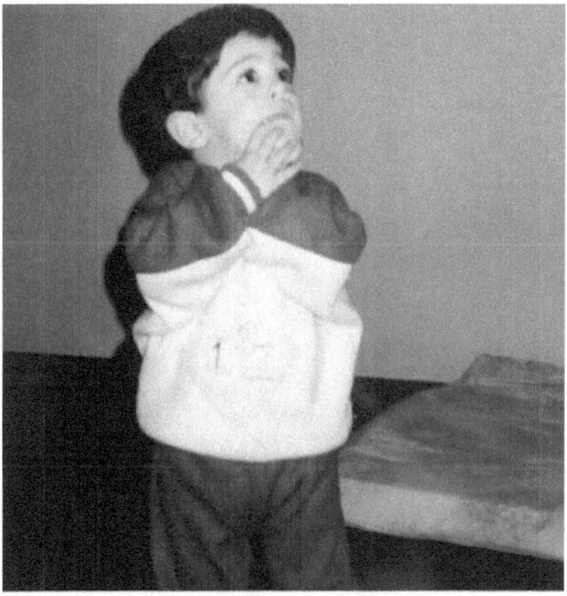

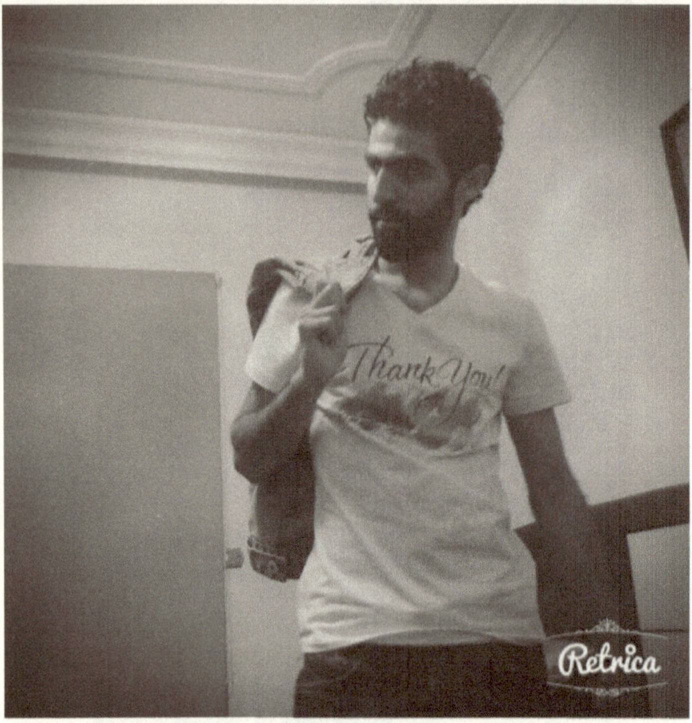
Thank You!
Retrica

BRASIL